Business Analytics for Beginners

By

Jaiden Dev

TABLE OF CONTENTS

INTRODUCTION

In today's fast-paced and data-driven world, businesses face an overwhelming amount of information. Extracting valuable insights from this sea of data has become crucial for organizations striving to make informed decisions, gain a competitive edge, and drive growth. This is where the power of business analytics comes into play.

Business Analytics for Beginners is an essential guide designed to demystify the world of analytics and equip you with the foundational knowledge and skills to navigate this dynamic field. Whether you're a business professional seeking to enhance your analytical capabilities or a student venturing into the world of data-driven decision-making, this book will serve as your comprehensive roadmap.

This book starts by unraveling the concept of business analytics, clarifying its purpose, and highlighting its immense significance in today's decision-making landscape. It explores the various types of analytics, including descriptive, diagnostic, predictive, and prescriptive analytics, helping you grasp the distinct roles each plays in transforming raw data into actionable insights.

Understanding the data itself is a crucial step, and the book delves into the intricacies of data collection and preparation. From identifying data sources and types to selecting appropriate collection methods, you will gain insights into the best practices of acquiring high-quality data. Additionally, the book guides you through the essential processes of data cleaning, preprocessing, and transformation to ensure reliable and accurate analytics outcomes.

Exploratory Data Analysis (EDA) serves as the gateway to uncovering patterns and trends within the data. This book equips you with a comprehensive understanding of EDA techniques and emphasizes the importance of visualization in unraveling insights that might otherwise remain hidden.

Statistical analysis plays a pivotal role in extracting meaning from data, and a solid foundation in statistical concepts from hypothesis testing to correlation and regression analysis, you will gain a clear understanding of how statistical methods contribute to informed decision-making. Time series analysis, a powerful tool for understanding and predicting trends in time-dependent data, is also explored in detail.

Predictive modeling takes center stage as you embark on your journey towards harnessing the power of machine learning algorithms. Feature selection and engineering are also covered, enabling you to extract the most relevant information from their data.

However, data and insights alone are not enough. Effective communication and visualization are essential to convey findings and recommendations. The book explores various visualization tools and techniques, emphasizing the art of designing informative and visually appealing dashboards that effectively communicate complex information to diverse stakeholders.

This book provides an overview of business intelligence, and its integration into the decision-making process. You will also gain insights into decision support systems and how they enable organizations to make strategic choices based on data-driven insights. Let's dive in!

CHAPTER 1

UNDERSTANDING BUSINESS ANALYTICS

1.1 Definition and Purpose of Business Analytics

Business analytics refers to the practice of analyzing data to derive meaningful insights and make informed business decisions. It involves the application of statistical and quantitative methods, data mining techniques, predictive modeling, and machine learning algorithms to interpret vast amounts of data and uncover patterns, trends, and correlations. Business analytics leverages both historical and real-time data to generate actionable insights that drive strategic, operational, and tactical decision-making within an organization.

Purpose of Business Analytics:

The purpose of business analytics is to enable organizations to gain a competitive advantage by making data-driven decisions. By harnessing the power of data, business analytics aims to improve business performance, enhance operational efficiency, optimize processes, identify new opportunities, mitigate risks, and enhance overall decision-making effectiveness. Here are some key purposes of business analytics:

a. Decision Making: Business analytics provides decision-makers with accurate and relevant information to support strategic, operational, and tactical decisions. It enables managers to make informed choices by providing insights into market trends, customer behavior, and operational performance.

b. Performance Measurement and Monitoring: Business analytics helps organizations measure and monitor their performance against key performance indicators (KPIs) and business objectives. By tracking and analyzing relevant metrics, businesses can identify areas for improvement, track progress, and take corrective actions as needed.

c. Predictive Analytics: Business analytics utilizes predictive modeling and advanced statistical techniques to forecast future outcomes and trends. By analyzing historical data and identifying patterns, organizations can make predictions about customer behavior, market demand, and other business variables, enabling proactive decision-making.

d. Customer Analytics: Understanding customers is vital for businesses to thrive. Business analytics helps organizations gain insights into customer preferences, behavior, and needs. This information can be used to personalize marketing campaigns, improve customer experience, and enhance customer retention strategies.

e. Operational Efficiency: Business analytics helps optimize operational processes by identifying bottlenecks, inefficiencies, and areas for improvement. By analyzing data related to resource allocation, supply chain management, and production processes, organizations can streamline operations, reduce costs, and enhance overall efficiency.

f. Risk Management: Business analytics enables organizations to identify and mitigate risks effectively. By analyzing historical data and employing predictive models, businesses can assess potential risks, such as fraud, market fluctuations, or supply chain disruptions, and develop strategies to minimize their impact.

g. Data-Driven Innovation: Business analytics fosters a culture of data-driven innovation within organizations. By exploring and analyzing data, businesses can uncover new opportunities, discover market trends, and develop innovative products and services to meet customer demands and gain a competitive edge.

Overall, business analytics is the systematic use of data analysis techniques to gain insights, drive informed decision-making, improve operational efficiency, mitigate risks, and foster innovation. It empowers organizations to harness the power of data and transform it into actionable intelligence for achieving their business goals.

1.2 Key Concepts in Business Analytics

Business analytics is a field that involves the use of data analysis and statistical methods to drive informed decision-making within organizations. Here are some key concepts in business analytics:

a. Data-driven decision-making: Business analytics emphasizes making decisions based on objective data rather than relying solely on intuition or gut feelings. By analyzing and interpreting data, organizations can gain valuable insights that help guide their strategic and operational choices.

b. Descriptive analytics: Descriptive analytics focuses on understanding what has happened in the past. It involves summarizing and visualizing historical data to identify patterns, trends, and relationships. Descriptive analytics answers questions like "What happened?" and "Why did it happen?"

c. Predictive analytics: Predictive analytics aims to forecast future outcomes based on historical data. By using statistical modeling and machine learning techniques, organizations can make predictions about customer behavior, market trends, and other variables. Predictive analytics helps answer questions like "What is likely to happen?" and "What if scenarios?"

d. Prescriptive analytics: Prescriptive analytics goes beyond prediction and provides recommendations on the best course of action. It leverages optimization models and algorithms to determine the optimal decision given specific constraints and objectives. Prescriptive analytics helps answer questions like "What should we do?" and "How can we achieve the best outcome?"

e. Data visualization: Data visualization is the graphical representation of data and information. It helps in presenting complex data sets in a visually appealing and easy-to-understand manner. Effective data visualization allows stakeholders to quickly grasp insights and make informed decisions.

f. Key performance indicators (KPIs): KPIs are quantifiable metrics that measure the performance and progress of an organization or specific activities. They help track important goals and objectives, enabling businesses to evaluate their performance and make data-driven improvements.

g. Data mining: Data mining involves the process of discovering patterns, relationships, and insights from large data sets. It utilizes various techniques, such as clustering, classification, and association analysis, to extract valuable information from data.

h. Machine learning: Machine learning is a subset of artificial intelligence that enables systems to automatically learn and improve from experience without being explicitly programmed. It uses algorithms to identify patterns in data and make predictions or take actions based on those patterns.

i. Data cleansing: Data cleansing, or data cleaning, is the process of identifying and correcting or removing errors, inconsistencies, and inaccuracies in data. It ensures that data is accurate, reliable, and suitable for analysis.

j. Business intelligence (BI): Business intelligence refers to the technologies, tools, and processes used to gather, analyze, and present business information. BI provides organizations with actionable insights and supports decision-making at various levels, from operational to strategic.

These key concepts form the foundation of business analytics and are crucial for organizations aiming to leverage data-driven insights to gain a competitive advantage and optimize their operations.

1.3 Importance of Business Analytics in Decision-Making

Business analytics plays a crucial role in decision-making for organizations across various industries. It involves the use of data, statistical models, and analytical techniques to extract valuable insights and make informed business decisions. Here are some key points explaining the importance of business analytics in decision-making:

a. Data-driven decision-making: In today's data-driven world, businesses have access to vast amounts of data. However, without effective analysis, this data remains underutilized. Business analytics enables organizations to leverage their data by uncovering patterns, trends, and correlations. These insights serve as a foundation for making informed decisions, rather than relying solely on intuition or guesswork.

b. Improved accuracy and efficiency: Business analytics provides a systematic and objective approach to decision-making. By analyzing historical data and using predictive modeling techniques, organizations can make accurate forecasts, identify potential risks, and evaluate the impact of different scenarios. This helps in optimizing processes, allocating resources effectively, and improving overall efficiency.

c. Identification of key performance indicators (KPIs): Business analytics helps in identifying and defining relevant KPIs that align with an organization's goals and objectives. By monitoring these KPIs, decision-makers can track performance, identify areas for improvement, and take timely corrective actions. Analytics also enables the identification of leading indicators, which provide early warnings about potential issues, allowing for proactive decision-making.

d. Competitive advantage: In today's competitive landscape, organizations need to differentiate themselves and stay ahead of the competition. Business analytics provides a competitive advantage by enabling organizations to uncover market trends, customer preferences, and emerging opportunities. By leveraging these insights, businesses can make strategic decisions to develop innovative products, tailor marketing strategies, and optimize their operations.

e. Risk management: Decision-making inherently involves risks, and business analytics helps in managing and mitigating these risks. By analyzing historical data and applying risk models, organizations can identify potential risks, assess their probability and impact, and develop risk mitigation strategies. Analytics also enables real-time monitoring of risk indicators, allowing for proactive decision-making to avoid or minimize potential negative outcomes.

f. Enhanced customer understanding: Business analytics helps in gaining a deep understanding of customers' preferences, behavior, and needs. By analyzing customer data, organizations can segment their customer base, identify target segments, and personalize their offerings. This leads to improved customer satisfaction, increased customer loyalty, and ultimately, higher revenues.

g. Resource optimization: Business analytics assists in optimizing the allocation of resources, such as finances, manpower, and inventory. By analyzing data on resource utilization, organizations can identify areas of inefficiency, reduce waste, and streamline operations. This optimization leads to cost savings, improved productivity, and increased profitability.

h. Agility and adaptability: In today's dynamic business environment, organizations need to be agile and adaptable to stay relevant. Business analytics provides real-time insights and enables organizations to respond quickly to market changes, customer demands, and emerging trends. This agility allows for faster decision-making, reducing the time lag between data analysis and action.

CHAPTER 2

TYPES OF BUSINESS ANALYTICS

2.1 Descriptive Analytics

Descriptive analytics is a branch of analytics that focuses on examining historical data to understand past patterns, trends, and events within a business or organization. It involves summarizing and organizing data in a meaningful way to gain insights into what has happened in the past.

The primary goal of descriptive analytics is to provide a clear picture of the current state of affairs and enable businesses to make informed decisions based on the available data. By analyzing historical data, businesses can identify patterns, correlations, and trends that can help them understand their customers, products, operations, and overall performance.

Descriptive analytics techniques involve various statistical and data visualization methods to explore and summarize data effectively. These methods may include measures such as central tendency (mean, median, mode), dispersion (range, standard deviation), frequency distributions, histograms, scatter plots, and more. These techniques help in gaining a comprehensive understanding of the data and uncovering important insights.

By leveraging descriptive analytics, businesses can answer questions like:

- What were the sales figures for a specific product last quarter?
- How many customers visited our website last month?
- What were the most popular products purchased during a particular period?
- What is the average time taken to resolve customer complaints?
- Which regions or customer segments have shown the highest growth rate?

Descriptive analytics serves as the foundation for further stages of analytics, such as predictive and prescriptive analytics. Once businesses have a clear understanding of historical data, they can leverage predictive analytics to forecast future outcomes and prescriptive analytics to recommend actions to optimize performance.

Overall, descriptive analytics is a crucial component of business analytics that focuses on analyzing historical data to gain insights into past trends and patterns. It provides businesses with a solid understanding of their current state, enabling them to make data-driven decisions and identify areas for improvement.

2.2 Diagnostic Analytics

Diagnostic analytics is a branch of business analytics that focuses on understanding the root causes of past events or outcomes. It involves the analysis of historical data to uncover patterns, trends, and relationships that explain why certain events occurred. Diagnostic analytics aims to provide insights into what happened, why it happened, and what factors contributed to the outcome.

The main objective of diagnostic analytics is to help organizations gain a deeper understanding of their business processes and make informed decisions based on data-driven insights. By identifying the factors that influenced past outcomes, companies can gain valuable insights into their operations, performance, and potential areas for improvement.

To perform diagnostic analytics, various techniques and tools can be employed. These include:

a. Data exploration: Exploring and visualizing data to identify patterns, correlations, and anomalies that may provide clues to the underlying causes of specific events.

b. Root cause analysis: Digging deeper into the data to identify the fundamental reasons behind specific outcomes. This involves investigating potential causal relationships and examining multiple variables to determine their impact on the observed results.

c. Statistical analysis: Applying statistical techniques to analyze data and test hypotheses about the relationships between different variables. Regression analysis, correlation analysis, and hypothesis testing are commonly used statistical methods in diagnostic analytics.

d. Data mining: Using advanced algorithms and techniques to extract useful information and uncover hidden patterns or relationships in large datasets. Data mining can help identify factors that contribute to specific outcomes and discover unexpected associations.

e. Comparative analysis: Comparing data across different periods, segments, or groups to identify variations and understand the factors that differentiate high-performing or successful instances from others.

f. Case studies and simulations: Studying real-life cases and conducting simulations to simulate different scenarios and assess the impact of various factors on outcomes. This helps in understanding the cause-and-effect relationships and predicting the consequences of different decisions or interventions.

The insights gained from diagnostic analytics can be valuable for decision-making, problem-solving, and performance improvement. By understanding the underlying causes of past events, organizations can take proactive measures to address issues, optimize processes, and drive better outcomes in the future.

Overall, diagnostic analytics plays a crucial role in helping businesses gain a deeper understanding of their data and derive actionable insights to improve performance, efficiency, and competitiveness.

2.3 Predictive Analytics

Predictive analytics is a branch of business analytics that utilizes statistical techniques, data mining, and machine learning algorithms to analyze historical and current data in order to make predictions about future events or outcomes. It aims to identify patterns, relationships, and trends in data that can be used to forecast future behaviors, events, or probabilities.

The process of predictive analytics typically involves several stages:

   a. Data collection: Relevant data from various sources, such as customer records, transactional data, social media data, or sensor data, is collected and compiled for analysis.

b. Data preprocessing: This stage involves cleaning and transforming the collected data to ensure its quality and consistency. Missing values may be imputed, outliers may be treated, and variables may be standardized or normalized.

c. Exploratory data analysis: Data is explored and visualized to gain insights into its characteristics, identify patterns, and detect any outliers or anomalies. This step helps in understanding the data and formulating hypotheses.

d. Feature selection/engineering: Relevant features or variables that are likely to have a significant impact on the prediction task are selected or engineered. This step aims to improve the model's accuracy and efficiency by focusing on the most important factors.

e. Model selection: Various predictive modeling techniques, such as regression analysis, decision trees, neural networks, or ensemble methods, are considered and evaluated based on the specific problem and data characteristics. The chosen model should be suitable for the problem at hand and capable of capturing the underlying relationships in the data.

f. Model training: The selected model is trained using historical data, where the input variables and corresponding known outcomes are used to learn the relationships between them. The model adjusts its parameters to minimize the prediction errors or maximize its performance on the training data.

g. Model evaluation: The trained model is evaluated using evaluation metrics and techniques such as cross-validation, where the model's performance is assessed on unseen data. This step helps to estimate how well the model is likely to perform on new data and identifies any potential issues like overfitting or underfitting.

h. Model deployment: Once the model has been trained and evaluated, it is deployed into the business environment, either as a standalone application or integrated into existing systems or processes. It starts making predictions on new, unseen data.

i. Monitoring and maintenance: Predictive models should be monitored regularly to ensure their accuracy and performance over time. As new data becomes available, the model may need retraining or updating to maintain its relevance and effectiveness.

Predictive analytics can be applied to a wide range of business applications, including customer segmentation, churn prediction, demand forecasting, fraud detection, risk assessment, inventory optimization, and personalized marketing. By leveraging historical and current data to anticipate future outcomes, businesses can make more informed decisions, optimize their operations, identify opportunities, and mitigate risks.

2.4 Prescriptive Analytics

Prescriptive analytics is a branch of business analytics that focuses on providing recommendations or prescriptions for optimal actions to be taken in order to achieve desired outcomes. It goes beyond descriptive analytics, which describes what has happened, and predictive analytics, which predicts what is likely to happen.

Prescriptive analytics utilizes advanced techniques such as optimization, simulation, and decision analysis to generate actionable insights. By considering various constraints, objectives, and possible actions, it helps businesses make informed decisions and take proactive measures to optimize their operations, improve efficiency, and maximize performance.

The main goal of prescriptive analytics is to answer the question, "What should we do?" It involves analyzing large volumes of data, including historical data, real-time data, and external data sources, to determine the best course of action in a given situation. This analysis involves identifying patterns, relationships, and dependencies in the data to uncover hidden insights and potential opportunities.

Prescriptive analytics typically follows a four-step process:

a. Define the objective: Clearly articulate the desired outcome or objective that the business wants to achieve. This could be maximizing profit, minimizing costs, optimizing resource allocation, or any other measurable goal.

b. Collect and analyze data: Gather relevant data from various sources, both internal and external. This may include customer data, market data, operational data, financial data, and more. Clean and preprocess the data, and then apply various analytical techniques to extract insights and identify potential actions.

c. Generate alternatives: Based on the analysis of the data, develop a set of potential actions or decisions that could be taken to achieve the defined objective. These alternatives should consider the constraints and limitations of the business, such as budgetary restrictions, operational capacity, regulatory requirements, and customer preferences.

d. Evaluate and implement: Evaluate each alternative based on predefined criteria and constraints. This involves simulating different scenarios, running optimization models, or performing sensitivity analyses to understand the potential outcomes of each decision. Finally, select the optimal course of action and implement it in the business operations.

Prescriptive analytics finds applications across various industries and business functions. It can help optimize supply chain management by determining the best inventory levels, production schedules, and distribution routes. In marketing, it can guide companies in making data-driven decisions on pricing, promotions, and customer segmentation. In finance, it can assist with portfolio optimization, risk management, and fraud detection.

Overall, prescriptive analytics empowers businesses to move beyond understanding and predicting past and future events. It enables them to make intelligent, data-driven decisions and take proactive actions to optimize their operations, improve efficiency, and achieve their strategic goals.

CHAPTER 3

DATA COLLECTION AND PREPARATION

3.1 Data Sources and Types

Data Sources:

Data sources refer to the places or systems from which we collect data for analysis. These sources can be classified into two main categories: internal and external.

I. Internal Data Sources: Internal data sources are the data generated within an organization or company. They include various systems and databases that store operational and transactional information. Some common internal data sources include customer relationship management (CRM) systems, enterprise resource planning (ERP) systems, sales databases, and financial records. Internal data sources are valuable as they contain specific and relevant information about the organization's operations, customers, and performance.

II. External Data Sources: External data sources are data obtained from outside the organization. These sources provide additional insights and context to complement internal data. External data sources can be categorized into several types:

a. Public Data Sources: These include government databases, open data initiatives, public surveys, and publicly available datasets. Examples include census data, economic indicators, weather data, and social media data.

b. Commercial Data Sources: These are third-party providers that offer specialized datasets for specific industries or purposes. Examples include market research firms, credit bureaus, and data aggregators. Commercial data sources can provide valuable market trends, consumer behavior data, and industry benchmarks.

c. Web Data: This refers to data collected from websites, web scraping, or application programming interfaces (APIs). It can include customer reviews, social media data, online user behavior, and website analytics.

d. Partners and Vendors: Data obtained from partners, vendors, or suppliers can be another valuable external data source. This can include data exchanged through collaborations, joint ventures, or supply chain systems.

e. Syndicated Data: Syndicated data refers to data collected and sold by specialized research companies. These companies collect data from various sources and provide industry-specific insights to multiple clients. Syndicated data can be particularly useful for market research and benchmarking purposes.

Data Types:

a. Data types refer to the nature or format of the data being collected, stored, and analyzed. Understanding data types is crucial as it determines the appropriate analysis techniques and tools.

b. Structured Data: Structured data is highly organized and follows a predefined format. It is typically stored in databases and spreadsheets. This type of data can be easily categorized, sorted, and analyzed using traditional database management systems. Examples of structured data include customer information, sales transactions, and financial statements.

c. Unstructured Data: Unstructured data is not organized in a predefined manner and lacks a specific format. It can come in various forms such as text documents, emails, social media posts, images, videos, and audio files. Analyzing unstructured data requires advanced techniques such as natural language processing, text mining, and image recognition.

d. Semi-Structured Data: Semi-structured data lies between structured and unstructured data. It contains some organizational elements but does not conform to a strict structure. Examples include XML files, JSON files, and log files. Semi-structured data often requires preprocessing and transformation before analysis.

e. Time-Series Data: Time-series data captures information over a specific period at regular intervals. It includes data points recorded at successive time points, such as stock prices, temperature readings, or website traffic data. Analyzing time-series data allows for trend analysis, forecasting, and anomaly detection.

f. Geospatial Data: Geospatial data contains information associated with specific geographic locations. It includes coordinates, maps, satellite imagery, and spatial databases. Geospatial data is commonly used in industries like logistics, urban planning, and environmental analysis.

g. Categorical Data: Categorical data represents qualitative or discrete variables. It includes data that falls into distinct categories or groups, such as gender, product categories, or customer segments. Categorical data is often represented as labels or codes and is analyzed using statistical techniques like frequency analysis, cross-tabulation, and chi-square tests.

h. Numerical Data: Numerical data represents quantitative variables that can be measured or counted. It includes continuous data, such as age, temperature, or sales revenue, as well as discrete data, such as the number of products sold or customer ratings. Numerical data allows for mathematical operations, statistical analysis, and visualization techniques like histograms and scatter plots.

i. Binary Data: Binary data represents variables with only two possible values, typically denoted as 0 and 1. It is commonly used in scenarios where a yes/no or true/false response is required. Examples of binary data include customer churn (1 for churned, 0 for not churned), fraud detection (1 for fraud, 0 for non-fraud), or the presence of a specific condition (1 for present, 0 for absent).

j. Ordinal Data: Ordinal data represents variables with an inherent order or ranking. The values have a meaningful sequence, but the differences between them may not be uniform or measurable. Examples include ratings or satisfaction levels (e.g., poor, fair, good, excellent) or educational levels (e.g., high school, bachelor's, master's, Ph.D.). Analyzing ordinal data often involves techniques like rank correlation and ordinal regression.

k. Ratio Data: Ratio data represents variables with a meaningful zero point and equal intervals between values. It allows for meaningful mathematical operations like addition, subtraction, multiplication, and division. Examples of ratio data include time duration, weight, height, or revenue. Ratio data can be analyzed using various statistical techniques, including mean, median, standard deviation, and regression analysis.

l. Qualitative Data: Qualitative data refers to non-numeric data that provides descriptive information or subjective characteristics. It includes text-based data, observations, interviews, focus group transcripts, or open-ended survey responses. Analyzing qualitative data involves techniques like thematic analysis, content analysis, or sentiment analysis to extract insights and patterns.

m. Quantitative Data: Quantitative data represents numeric data that can be measured or counted. It includes numerical measurements, statistics, or numerical responses from surveys. Quantitative data allows for mathematical operations and statistical analysis to identify patterns, trends, and relationships.

Understanding the various data sources and types is essential for effective business analytics. It helps organizations identify the most relevant and reliable data sources and select appropriate analysis techniques to derive meaningful insights. By leveraging the right data sources and types, businesses can make data-driven decisions, gain a competitive edge, and uncover opportunities for growth and optimization.

3.2 Data Collection Methods

Data collection methods refer to the processes and techniques employed to gather relevant data for business analytics. These methods are crucial for acquiring accurate and reliable information that can be used to drive informed decision-making and gain insights into various aspects of a business.

a. Surveys and Questionnaires: Surveys involve collecting data through a series of structured questions presented to a target audience. They can be conducted in person, over the phone, through email, or online. Questionnaires follow a similar approach but can be self-administered. Surveys and questionnaires are effective for gathering subjective opinions, preferences, and demographic information.

b. Interviews: Interviews involve direct interaction between a researcher and an individual or a group. They can be structured (using predefined questions) or unstructured (allowing for open-ended discussions). Interviews are useful for obtaining detailed insights, clarifying responses, and exploring complex topics. They can be conducted face-to-face, via phone, or through video conferencing.

c. Observations: This method involves systematically observing and recording data about people, processes, or events in their natural settings.

It can be done overtly (where participants are aware of being observed) or covertly (where participants are unaware). Observations are valuable for capturing actual behavior and uncovering patterns that may not be apparent through other methods. It is commonly used in fields like retail, manufacturing, and customer behavior analysis.

d. Experiments: Experiments involve manipulating variables under controlled conditions to determine cause-and-effect relationships. They are commonly used in scientific research but can also be applied in business analytics. Experiments can be conducted in a laboratory or real-world setting. By comparing a control group with one or more experimental groups, insights can be gained into the impact of specific interventions or changes.

e. Secondary Data Collection: Secondary data refers to existing data collected by others for different purposes. This data can be obtained from internal sources (such as company records, databases, and reports) or external sources (such as government publications, industry reports, or research studies). Secondary data collection is advantageous as it is often easily accessible, cost-effective, and can provide historical context or benchmarks.

f. Web Scraping: Web scraping involves automatically extracting data from websites. This method is useful for gathering large amounts of data from multiple sources quickly. However, it is important to comply with legal and ethical guidelines when performing web scraping, respecting the terms of service and privacy policies of the websites being scraped.

g. Social Media Monitoring: Social media platforms generate vast amounts of user-generated data, including opinions, sentiments, and trends. Monitoring social media can provide valuable insights into customer preferences, brand perception, and emerging issues. Tools and algorithms can be used to collect and analyze data from platforms like Twitter, Facebook, Instagram, and LinkedIn.

h. Sensor Data Collection: In certain industries, sensor technologies are employed to collect real-time data. For example, in manufacturing, sensors can monitor machine performance or detect quality defects. In logistics, sensors can track shipments and monitor temperature or humidity. Sensor data collection enables continuous monitoring and helps identify patterns, anomalies, or potential improvements.

When choosing data collection methods, consider factors such as the research objectives, target audience, available resources, time constraints, and the nature of the data being collected.

Employing a combination of methods often yields a comprehensive and reliable dataset for business analytics purposes.

3.3 Data Cleaning and Preprocessing

Data cleaning and preprocessing are essential steps in the field of business analytics. They involve transforming raw data into a clean and structured format that can be analyzed effectively. This process helps improve the quality and reliability of the data, ensuring accurate and meaningful insights.

Data cleaning refers to the identification and correction of errors, inconsistencies, and inaccuracies in the dataset. Raw data often contains missing values, outliers, duplicate records, and formatting issues, which can negatively impact the analysis if not addressed properly.

To begin the data cleaning process, it is crucial to understand the dataset thoroughly. This includes examining the data structure, variable types, and any known data quality issues. Identifying missing values is a common challenge, as they can skew the analysis and lead to biased results. Different approaches can be used to handle missing data, such as imputation techniques where missing values are estimated based on available information or removing records with missing values, depending on the situation.

Outliers, which are data points that deviate significantly from the overall pattern, also need to be addressed during data cleaning. Outliers can arise due to measurement errors, data entry mistakes, or genuine extreme observations. They can have a disproportionate impact on statistical models and analysis. Various techniques like the use of statistical measures, visualization tools, or robust statistical models can help identify and handle outliers appropriately.

Duplicate records pose another challenge in data cleaning. These are repeated instances of the same data, which can occur due to system errors, merging data from different sources, or human error during data entry. Removing duplicates is important to ensure that the analysis is not skewed by redundant information. Techniques such as deduplication algorithms or matching criteria can be used to identify and eliminate duplicate records.

Data formatting issues are also common and can affect the accuracy and consistency of the analysis. These issues may include inconsistent date formats, different units of measurement, or varying coding schemes. Standardizing the data format helps ensure consistency and comparability across the dataset. This may involve converting data types, normalizing numerical values, or harmonizing categorical variables.

Once the data cleaning phase is complete, the next step is data preprocessing. This involves transforming the cleaned data into a format suitable for analysis and modeling. Preprocessing techniques can include feature scaling, dimensionality reduction, and feature engineering.

Feature scaling is applied when variables have different scales or units. It ensures that each variable contributes proportionally to the analysis by scaling them to a common range. Common techniques for feature scaling include normalization (scaling variables to a specific range) and standardization (transforming variables to have zero mean and unit variance).

Dimensionality reduction techniques are used when the dataset has a large number of variables, and there is a need to reduce the dimensionality for easier analysis. Techniques such as principal component analysis (PCA) or feature selection methods can help identify and retain the most informative variables while reducing computational complexity.

Feature engineering involves creating new variables or transforming existing ones to extract more meaningful information. This can include creating interaction terms, polynomial features, or aggregating variables to derive useful insights. Feature engineering aims to enhance the predictive power of the data and improve the performance of machine learning models.

Overall, data cleaning and preprocessing are crucial stages in business analytics. They involve identifying and addressing data quality issues, such as missing values, outliers, duplicates, and formatting problems. Once the data is cleaned, preprocessing techniques are applied to transform the data into a suitable format for analysis. These steps ensure that the data is accurate, reliable, and ready for further analysis and modeling, ultimately leading to more accurate insights and better decision-making.

3.4 Data Transformation and Integration

Data transformation and integration are crucial processes in the field of business analytics. They involve converting and merging data from various sources into a standardized format, making it suitable for analysis and decision-making. These processes play a vital role in extracting valuable insights, identifying patterns, and making informed business decisions.

Data transformation refers to the process of converting raw data into a consistent format that can be easily analyzed. This step often involves data cleaning, normalization, aggregation, and enrichment. Let's delve into each of these aspects:

a. Data Cleaning: This involves identifying and correcting errors, inconsistencies, and inaccuracies within the dataset. It includes tasks such as removing duplicates, handling missing values, and resolving discrepancies.

b. Data Normalization: Data often comes from different sources with varying formats, units, and structures. Normalization ensures that the data is standardized, allowing for meaningful comparisons and analysis. It typically involves transforming data into a common scale or range.

c. Data Aggregation: Aggregation involves combining multiple data points or records into a summarized representation. It helps in reducing data volume, simplifying analysis, and providing a higher-level view of the data. Aggregation can be performed by grouping data based on specific attributes and calculating summary statistics such as sums, averages, or counts.

d. Data Enrichment: Data enrichment involves enhancing the dataset with additional information that can provide context or improve analysis. This can include merging data from external sources, appending demographic information, or enriching data with calculated metrics or derived variables.

On the other hand, data integration focuses on combining data from different sources or systems to create a unified and comprehensive view. It aims to resolve data silos and ensure data consistency across the organization. Data integration can be achieved through various methods, including:

a. ETL (Extract, Transform, Load): ETL processes involve extracting data from source systems, transforming it into a consistent format, and loading it into a target system or data warehouse. This method is commonly used when dealing with large volumes of data or complex data structures.

b. API Integration: Application Programming Interfaces (APIs) allow different software applications to communicate and share data. API integration enables real-time or near-real-time data exchange between systems, eliminating the need for manual data transfer.

c. Data Virtualization: This approach involves creating a virtual layer that provides a unified view of data from multiple sources without physically integrating them.

It allows for on-demand access to data from disparate sources, minimizing data redundancy.

The benefits of data transformation and integration include:

a. Improved Data Quality: By cleaning, normalizing, and aggregating data, the overall quality and consistency of the dataset are enhanced. This leads to more accurate and reliable analysis results.

b. Enhanced Decision-making: Transforming and integrating data from different sources enables a holistic view of the business, leading to better-informed decision-making. It enables businesses to identify trends, patterns, and correlations that may not be apparent when analyzing data in isolation.

c. Efficient Reporting and Analysis: Standardizing data formats and structures simplifies reporting and analysis processes. It reduces the time and effort required to combine and analyze data from multiple sources, enabling analysts to focus on extracting insights rather than data preparation.

d. Integrated Systems and Processes: Data integration facilitates seamless data flow between systems, enabling efficient business operations. It allows for better synchronization of processes, streamlined workflows, and improved collaboration across departments.

Overall, data transformation and integration are fundamental processes in business analytics. They involve converting raw data into a consistent format and combining data from various sources to enable meaningful analysis and decision-making. These processes improve data quality, enhance decision-making, streamline operations, and ultimately contribute to business success.

CHAPTER 4

EXPLORATORY DATA ANALYSIS

4.1 Overview of Exploratory Data Analysis (EDA)

Exploratory Data Analysis (EDA) is a crucial step in the data analysis process, allowing business analysts to understand and explore the underlying patterns, relationships, and distributions within a dataset. EDA helps in extracting meaningful insights, identifying data quality issues, and forming hypotheses for further analysis. In this section, we'll delve into the key components and techniques used in EDA.

a. Data Collection and Familiarization:
   The first step in EDA is obtaining the dataset of interest and becoming familiar with its structure, variables, and data types. This involves understanding the data sources, data collection methods, and any relevant metadata associated with the dataset.

b. Data Cleaning and Preprocessing:
   Data cleaning is essential for handling missing values, outliers, inconsistent data formats, and resolving any other data quality issues. This process ensures the data is accurate and suitable for analysis. Preprocessing tasks may involve data imputation, normalization, encoding categorical variables, and feature scaling.

c. Univariate Analysis:

Univariate analysis focuses on examining individual variables in isolation. It involves summarizing and visualizing the distribution of a single variable using descriptive statistics, histograms, box plots, or density plots. This analysis helps identify outliers, understand the central tendency, and uncover patterns or anomalies within a variable.

d. Bivariate and Multivariate Analysis:

Bivariate analysis explores relationships between two variables, while multivariate analysis involves examining associations among multiple variables. Techniques such as scatter plots, correlation matrices, heatmaps, and pair plots aid in visualizing these relationships. These analyses reveal dependencies, correlations, and potential predictive features within the dataset.

e. Data Visualization:

EDA heavily relies on visualizations to effectively communicate patterns and insights. Visualizations such as bar charts, line plots, pie charts, histograms, box plots, scatter plots, and heatmaps help in understanding distributions, trends, clusters, and relationships within the data. Visualization tools and libraries like Matplotlib, Seaborn, and Plotly are commonly used.

f. Feature Engineering:
Feature engineering involves creating new derived features or transforming existing features to enhance the predictive power of a machine learning model. EDA plays a vital role in identifying potential features or combinations of features that may have a significant impact on the target variable. Techniques like one-hot encoding, scaling, discretization, and creating interaction variables can be employed.

g. Statistical Analysis and Hypothesis Testing:
EDA often includes statistical analysis to validate assumptions and test hypotheses. Techniques such as t-tests, ANOVA, chi-square tests, and correlation tests help in assessing the statistical significance of relationships between variables. These tests aid in decision-making and provide insights into the significance of various factors in the dataset.

h. Data Summary and Insights:
Finally, EDA culminates in summarizing the key findings, insights, and recommendations derived from the analysis. This may involve documenting observations, patterns, trends, and notable relationships discovered during the exploratory phase. These insights provide a foundation for further analysis, modeling, and decision-making processes.

Overall, Exploratory Data Analysis is a fundamental step in the data analysis pipeline. By employing various techniques and visualizations, analysts gain a deeper understanding of the dataset, identify data quality issues, uncover patterns, and generate hypotheses. EDA sets the stage for subsequent data modeling, predictive analytics, and decision-making tasks, enabling businesses to make data-driven decisions.

4.2 Techniques for EDA

Exploratory Data Analysis (EDA) is a critical step in the data analysis process, where you examine and visualize the data to gain insights and understand its underlying patterns and relationships. EDA techniques help uncover key characteristics, detect anomalies, and identify potential trends or patterns within the data.

Here are several techniques commonly used in EDA:

a. Summary Statistics: This technique involves calculating descriptive statistics such as mean, median, mode, standard deviation, minimum, and maximum. Summary statistics provide a quick overview of the data distribution and central tendencies, enabling analysts to understand the dataset's basic properties.

b. Data Visualization: Visualizing data through charts, graphs, and plots is a powerful EDA technique. It helps in understanding patterns, trends, and outliers more intuitively. Common visualizations include histograms, box plots, scatter plots, line charts, bar graphs, and heatmaps. These visual representations aid in identifying relationships between variables, spotting outliers, and assessing data distributions.

c. Data Cleaning: EDA often requires cleaning the data to address missing values, outliers, inconsistencies, and other data quality issues. Techniques like imputation, where missing values are estimated or replaced, and outlier detection and treatment, which involve identifying and handling extreme values, help ensure the integrity and reliability of the data.

d. Univariate Analysis: Univariate analysis focuses on analyzing a single variable in isolation. It involves computing summary statistics, visualizing the variable's distribution, and identifying outliers. Univariate techniques such as frequency distributions, histograms, and bar plots provide insights into individual variables' characteristics, helping to understand their range, spread, and central tendencies.

e. Bivariate Analysis: Bivariate analysis explores relationships between two variables. By examining the correlation or association between variables, analysts can uncover patterns and dependencies. Techniques like scatter plots, correlation matrices, and cross-tabulation help identify relationships, dependencies, and potential cause-and-effect dynamics between variables.

f. Multivariate Analysis: Multivariate analysis considers relationships between multiple variables simultaneously. Techniques like dimensionality reduction (e.g., principal component analysis) and clustering aid in understanding complex interactions and patterns within the data. Multivariate techniques enable analysts to identify groups or clusters of similar observations and detect hidden patterns that may not be apparent in univariate or bivariate analyses.

g. Time Series Analysis: Time series analysis is used when data is collected over time. It helps identify trends, seasonality, and patterns within the temporal dimension. Techniques such as line plots, autocorrelation, and decomposition assist in understanding the data's temporal behavior and can be used to forecast future values.

h. Hypothesis Testing: Hypothesis testing allows analysts to make inferences and draw conclusions about the data. It involves formulating a hypothesis, selecting an appropriate statistical test, and evaluating the evidence against the null hypothesis. Hypothesis testing helps validate or refute assumptions, investigate relationships, and determine the statistical significance of findings.

i. Data Segmentation: Data segmentation involves dividing the dataset into meaningful subsets based on specific criteria. This technique allows for a more detailed analysis of different segments and the comparison of their characteristics. Segmentation can be performed based on demographic variables, geographic regions, customer segments, or any other relevant factors that help partition the data.

Overall, employing these techniques for EDA enables you to uncover insights, identify data quality issues, explore relationships, and prepare the data for subsequent analysis. It serves as a foundation for further modeling, predictive analytics, and decision-making processes within an organization.

4.3 Visualization in EDA

Visualization plays a crucial role in Exploratory Data Analysis (EDA) as it enables business analysts to gain meaningful insights from complex datasets. EDA involves examining and understanding the data before applying any formal statistical techniques or modeling. By using visual representations of the data, analysts can uncover patterns, trends, and outliers that might not be apparent in raw data alone.

One of the primary purposes of visualization in EDA is to summarize and present data in a clear and concise manner. Visualizations, such as charts, graphs, and plots, help in understanding the distribution, central tendencies, and variations within the data. For example, a histogram can provide an overview of the frequency distribution of a continuous variable, while a box plot can show the quartiles, outliers, and median of a dataset.

Moreover, visualizations facilitate the identification of relationships and correlations between variables. Scatter plots are commonly used to visualize the relationship between two continuous variables, allowing analysts to assess whether there is a positive, negative, or no association between them. Similarly, heatmaps can display the correlations between multiple variables, providing a quick overview of the strength and direction of relationships.

Visualization also aids in detecting anomalies or outliers in the data. These are data points that deviate significantly from the expected patterns and can be crucial in identifying errors, data quality issues, or interesting observations. By using techniques like scatter plots, box plots, or violin plots, analysts can easily spot data points that lie far outside the normal range.

Another important aspect of visualization in EDA is the ability to explore data from different perspectives or dimensions. By leveraging interactive visualizations, analysts can dynamically interact with the data, filter subsets, and drill down into specific aspects of interest. This flexibility allows for a more comprehensive exploration of the data and enhances the discovery of hidden insights.

Additionally, visualizations are valuable in communicating findings and insights to stakeholders or non-technical audiences. Complex data can be overwhelming, and visual representations simplify the presentation of information, making it more accessible and understandable. By using visualizations in reports, presentations, or dashboards, analysts can effectively convey their findings, support decision-making, and drive actions based on data-driven insights.

Overall, visualization plays a critical role in EDA. Visualizations summarize data, identify patterns and relationships, detect anomalies, and facilitate multidimensional exploration. They also serve as powerful communication tools, enabling analysts to present their findings in a clear and compelling manner.

CHAPTER 5

STATISTICAL ANALYSIS FOR BUSINESS ANALYTICS

5.1 Statistical Concepts for Business Analytics

Statistical concepts play a crucial role in business analytics, providing the foundation for making data-driven decisions and extracting meaningful insights from large datasets. In this section, let's explore some key statistical concepts for business analytics.

a. Descriptive Statistics: Descriptive statistics involve summarizing and describing the main characteristics of a dataset. Measures such as mean, median, mode, standard deviation, and range are used to understand the central tendency, variability, and distribution of the data. Descriptive statistics help in gaining an initial understanding of the data and identifying patterns or outliers.

b. Probability: Probability theory is fundamental to business analytics as it deals with uncertainty and the likelihood of events occurring. Businesses often encounter uncertain situations, and probability helps quantify the chances of different outcomes. Concepts like probability distributions, random variables, and conditional probability enable analysts to make informed decisions under uncertainty.

c. Hypothesis Testing: Hypothesis testing is used to assess the validity of assumptions or claims about a population based on sample data. It involves formulating a null hypothesis and an alternative hypothesis, collecting sample data, and using statistical tests to determine if there is enough evidence to support or reject the null hypothesis. Hypothesis testing enables businesses to make inferences about populations based on limited sample data.

d. Regression Analysis: Regression analysis is a statistical technique used to model the relationship between a dependent variable and one or more independent variables. It helps identify the impact of different factors on a specific outcome and make predictions or estimations. Linear regression, logistic regression, and time series regression are commonly used regression techniques in business analytics.

e. Sampling Techniques: Sampling is the process of selecting a subset of individuals or items from a larger population to infer conclusions about the entire population. Various sampling techniques, such as simple random sampling, stratified sampling, and cluster sampling, are employed to ensure that the selected sample is representative of the population. Proper sampling techniques help minimize bias and enhance the accuracy of statistical analysis.

f. Time Series Analysis: Time series analysis is used to analyze data collected over time to identify patterns, trends, and seasonality. It involves techniques like smoothing, decomposition, autocorrelation, and forecasting. Time series analysis is particularly relevant in business analytics for forecasting sales, demand, stock prices, and other time-dependent variables.

g. Statistical Modeling: Statistical modeling involves developing mathematical models to represent relationships between variables based on observed data. It helps businesses understand the underlying factors that influence outcomes and make predictions or estimations. Techniques such as linear regression, logistic regression, and decision trees are commonly used for statistical modeling in business analytics.

h. Data Visualization: While not strictly a statistical concept, data visualization is an essential aspect of business analytics. Visualizing data using charts, graphs, and interactive dashboards helps communicate complex statistical findings in a clear and intuitive manner. It enables businesses to gain insights quickly, spot trends or anomalies, and make informed decisions.

By leveraging these statistical concepts, business analysts can effectively analyze data, draw meaningful conclusions, and derive actionable insights to drive decision-making and improve business performance.

5.2 Hypothesis Testing

Hypothesis testing is a statistical method used in business analytics to make decisions or draw conclusions about a population based on sample data. It involves formulating two competing hypotheses, the null hypothesis (H0) and the alternative hypothesis (Ha), and using statistical tests to determine the likelihood of observing the sample data if the null hypothesis were true.

The null hypothesis represents the default position or the claim that there is no significant difference or relationship between variables in the population. The alternative hypothesis, on the other hand, represents the claim that there is a significant difference or relationship.

The hypothesis testing process typically involves the following steps:

a. State the null and alternative hypotheses: The null hypothesis is usually stated as an equality or no difference, while the alternative hypothesis states the desired difference or relationship.

b. Select a significance level: The significance level, denoted by α, determines the threshold for accepting or rejecting the null hypothesis. Commonly used values for α are 0.05 or 0.01, representing a 5% or 1% chance of rejecting the null hypothesis incorrectly.

c. Choose an appropriate test statistic: The choice of test statistic depends on the nature of the data and the hypotheses being tested. Examples of commonly used test statistics include t-tests, chi-square tests, ANOVA, or regression analysis.

d. Collect and analyze the sample data: Data is collected from a representative sample of the population of interest. The sample data is then used to calculate the test statistic.

e. Calculate the p-value: The p-value is the probability of obtaining a test statistic as extreme as or more extreme than the observed value, assuming that the null hypothesis is true. A small p-value indicates strong evidence against the null hypothesis.

f. Make a decision: If the p-value is less than the chosen significance level, typically α, the null hypothesis is rejected in favor of the alternative hypothesis. Otherwise, the null hypothesis is not rejected.

g. Draw conclusions: Based on the decision made, conclusions can be drawn about the population. If the null hypothesis is rejected, it suggests evidence of a significant difference or relationship between variables.

Hypothesis testing helps businesses make data-driven decisions by providing a systematic framework for evaluating claims or hypotheses. It allows them to assess the effectiveness of marketing campaigns, compare product performance, analyze customer preferences, and evaluate the impact of interventions or process improvements, among other applications. By using hypothesis testing, businesses can reduce uncertainty and make informed decisions based on statistical evidence.

5.3 Correlation and Regression Analysis

Correlation and regression analysis are statistical techniques used in business analytics to examine the relationships between variables and make predictions or forecast future outcomes. Let's delve into these concepts in detail:

Correlation Analysis:

Correlation analysis is used to measure the strength and direction of the relationship between two variables. It helps determine whether a change in one variable is associated with a change in another variable. The correlation coefficient, usually denoted as "r," ranges between -1 and +1.

A positive correlation (r > 0) indicates that as one variable increases, the other variable tends to increase as well. For example, there may be a positive correlation between advertising expenditure and sales revenue.

A negative correlation (r < 0) implies that as one variable increases, the other variable tends to decrease. An example could be the correlation between product price and customer demand.

A correlation coefficient of zero (r = 0) suggests no linear relationship between the variables. However, it's important to note that there might still exist a non-linear relationship between them.

It's essential to understand that correlation does not imply causation. Even if two variables are strongly correlated, it does not necessarily mean that one variable is causing the change in the other. Correlation merely indicates a statistical relationship.

Regression Analysis:

Regression analysis is a statistical technique used to model the relationship between a dependent variable and one or more independent variables. It enables us to predict the value of the dependent variable based on the values of the independent variables.

There are different types of regression analysis, but the most common one is simple linear regression, which involves a single dependent variable and one independent variable. The relationship between these variables is represented by a straight-line equation, typically in the form of:

$$Y = b0 + b1*X + \varepsilon$$

Here, Y represents the dependent variable, X is the independent variable, b0 is the intercept or constant term, b1 is the regression coefficient (slope), and ε represents the error term.

The regression coefficient (b1) indicates how much the dependent variable is expected to change when the independent variable changes by one unit, assuming all other variables remain constant. The intercept (b0) represents the value of the dependent variable when the independent variable is zero.

Regression analysis provides insights into the strength and significance of the relationship between variables. It also helps in making predictions or estimating the impact of changes in the independent variable on the dependent variable.

Furthermore, regression analysis can be extended to multiple regression, where more than one independent variable is used to predict the dependent variable. This allows for examining the influence of multiple factors simultaneously.

Overall, correlation analysis assesses the relationship between variables, while regression analysis models and predicts the dependent variable based on independent variables. Both techniques are valuable tools for business analytics, enabling businesses to gain insights, make informed decisions, and forecast future outcomes based on data analysis.

5.4 Time Series Analysis

Time series analysis is a statistical technique used to analyze and forecast data that changes over time. It is widely used in business analytics to understand patterns, trends, and seasonality in data to make informed decisions and predictions.

The fundamental concept behind time series analysis is that the data points are ordered chronologically, and each observation is dependent on previous observations. This temporal dependency allows us to study the historical behavior of the data and use it to predict future values.

There are several key components in time series analysis:

a. Trend: Trend refers to the long-term upward or downward movement in the data. It helps identify the overall direction in which the data is moving and can be linear or nonlinear.

b. Seasonality: Seasonality represents regular patterns or cycles that occur within a specific time frame, such as daily, weekly, or yearly. For example, retail sales may exhibit higher peaks during holiday seasons each year.

c. Cyclicity: Cyclicity refers to longer-term patterns or cycles that are not as regular as seasonality. These cycles may occur over several years or decades, such as economic recessions or booms.

d. Irregularity: Irregular or random fluctuations in the data that cannot be attributed to trends, seasonality, or cyclical patterns. They represent noise or unpredictable factors affecting the data.

To analyze a time series, various statistical techniques can be applied, including:

a. Descriptive statistics: These involve calculating summary statistics such as mean, median, standard deviation, and percentiles to understand the central tendency, dispersion, and shape of the data.

b. Smoothing: Smoothing techniques, such as moving averages or exponential smoothing, are used to remove noise and reveal underlying trends or patterns in the data.

c. Decomposition: Decomposition separates a time series into its individual components, such as trend, seasonality, cyclicity, and irregularity. This helps isolate and understand each component's contribution to the overall behavior of the series.

d. Autocorrelation: Autocorrelation measures the relationship between a data point and its lagged values. It helps identify if there is a correlation between past observations and the current value, which is essential for understanding and modeling time-dependent patterns.

e. Forecasting: Time series forecasting involves predicting future values based on historical patterns. Techniques like ARIMA (Autoregressive Integrated Moving

Average), exponential smoothing, and machine learning algorithms can be used for forecasting.

Time series analysis finds applications in various business areas, including demand forecasting, sales forecasting, stock market analysis, economic forecasting, supply chain optimization, and anomaly detection. By understanding and predicting the behavior of time-dependent data, businesses can make more informed decisions, allocate resources effectively, and improve their overall performance.

Overall, time series analysis is a powerful tool for understanding and forecasting data that changes over time. It helps businesses gain insights into patterns, trends, and seasonality, enabling them to make data-driven decisions and improve their operations and planning.

CHAPTER 6

PREDICTIVE MODELING

6.1 Introduction to Predictive Modeling

Predictive modeling is a powerful technique used in business analytics to analyze historical data and make predictions or forecasts about future outcomes. It involves building mathematical models based on past observations to predict unknown future events or behaviors. Predictive models are widely employed across various industries to gain insights, make informed decisions, and improve business performance.

The goal of predictive modeling is to develop accurate and reliable models that can anticipate future events with a reasonable level of certainty. These models can be applied to a wide range of business scenarios, such as sales forecasting, customer behavior analysis, risk assessment, demand prediction, fraud detection, and many more.

The predictive modeling process typically involves several steps:

a. Problem Definition: Clearly define the business problem or question you want to address through predictive modeling. Identify the specific outcome you want to predict, such as sales volume, customer churn, or product demand.

b. Data Collection: Gather relevant data that is representative of the problem at hand. This data can include historical records, customer demographics, transactional data, marketing campaigns, online interactions, and any other relevant information.

c. Data Preprocessing: Clean and prepare the collected data for analysis. This involves handling missing values, outliers, and inconsistencies, as well as transforming variables and performing feature engineering to create meaningful predictors for the predictive model.

d. Exploratory Data Analysis (EDA): Conduct a thorough analysis of the data to gain insights and identify patterns or relationships. EDA helps in understanding the data distribution, correlations, and potential variables that might impact the outcome.

e. Model Selection: Choose an appropriate predictive modeling technique based on the problem and data characteristics. Common techniques include linear regression, logistic regression, decision trees, random forests, support vector machines, neural networks, and ensemble methods.

f. Model Training: Split the available data into training and validation sets. Use the training set to train the predictive model by fitting the chosen algorithm to the data, optimizing model parameters, and minimizing prediction errors.

g. Model Evaluation: Assess the performance of the trained model using the validation set. Common evaluation metrics include accuracy, precision, recall, F1 score, area under the receiver operating characteristic curve (AUC-ROC), and mean squared error (MSE), depending on the nature of the problem.

h. Model Deployment: Once the predictive model has demonstrated satisfactory performance, it can be deployed in a production environment for making predictions on new, unseen data. Integration with existing business systems or processes may be necessary for seamless implementation.

i. Model Monitoring and Maintenance: Regularly monitor the performance of the deployed model to ensure its continued accuracy and relevance. As new data becomes available, retraining the model periodically or updating it with additional data may be required to maintain its effectiveness.

Predictive modeling offers several benefits to businesses. It enables proactive decision-making, identifies potential risks, optimizes resource allocation, improves marketing campaigns, enhances customer segmentation, streamlines inventory management, and drives overall business efficiency and profitability.

Overall, predictive modeling is a valuable tool in business analytics that leverages historical data to make informed predictions about future outcomes. By following a systematic modeling process, businesses can unlock valuable insights and gain a competitive advantage in an increasingly data-driven world.

6.2 Machine Learning Algorithms for Predictive Modeling

Machine learning algorithms play a crucial role in predictive modeling, enabling businesses to extract insights from data and make accurate predictions. These algorithms employ statistical techniques to learn patterns and relationships within the data and use them to make predictions or classifications on new, unseen data. Here, I'll explain some commonly used machine learning algorithms for predictive modeling.

a. Linear Regression: Linear regression is a fundamental algorithm used for predicting a continuous outcome variable based on one or more input variables. It assumes a linear relationship between the input variables and the target variable, fitting a line that best represents the data.

b. Logistic Regression: Unlike linear regression, logistic regression is used for binary classification problems where the target variable has two possible outcomes. It estimates the probability of an event occurring based on the input variables and applies a logistic function to make predictions.

c. Decision Trees: Decision trees are tree-like structures that make predictions by partitioning the data into smaller subsets based on different attribute values. These splits are determined by evaluating the significance of variables in predicting the target variable. Decision trees are easy to interpret but can be prone to overfitting.

d. Random Forest: A random forest is an ensemble method that combines multiple decision trees to make predictions. It creates a collection of decision trees and uses their combined outputs to generate the final prediction. Random forests reduce overfitting and improve prediction accuracy by introducing randomness during tree construction.

e. Gradient Boosting: Gradient boosting is another ensemble technique that builds an ensemble of weak prediction models, typically decision trees, in a sequential manner. Each subsequent model is trained to correct the errors made by the previous models, resulting in a strong predictive model.

Gradient boosting is known for its high accuracy and ability to handle complex relationships.

f. Support Vector Machines (SVM): SVM is a versatile algorithm used for both regression and classification tasks. It maps the input data into a high-dimensional feature space and finds the optimal hyperplane that separates different classes or predicts continuous values with the maximum margin.

g. Neural Networks: Neural networks are a class of algorithms inspired by the human brain's structure and function. They consist of interconnected nodes or "neurons" organized in layers. Neural networks excel in capturing complex patterns and relationships, making them suitable for various predictive modeling tasks.

h. Naive Bayes: Naive Bayes is a probabilistic algorithm based on Bayes' theorem. It assumes independence between features and calculates the probability of a particular class given the feature values. Despite its simplistic assumptions, Naive Bayes performs well in many real-world applications.

i. K-Nearest Neighbors (KNN): KNN is a simple yet powerful algorithm that predicts the class or value of a new data point based on its proximity to the k-nearest neighbors in the training set. It measures distance between data points and assigns the majority class or average value of the k-nearest neighbors.

These are just a few examples of machine learning algorithms commonly used for predictive modeling. The choice of algorithm depends on various factors such as the nature of the problem, the availability of data, the interpretability requirements, and the trade-off between accuracy and computation time. It's important to experiment with different algorithms and fine-tune their parameters to achieve the best predictive performance for a given task.

6.3 Model Evaluation and Validation

Model evaluation and validation are essential steps in the data modeling process. They involve assessing the performance and reliability of a predictive or analytical model before deploying it in a real-world business environment. These steps are crucial to ensure that the model can make accurate and reliable predictions or provide valuable insights.

The model evaluation process begins by dividing the available dataset into two main subsets: the training set and the testing set. The training set is used to develop and train the model, while the testing set is used to evaluate its performance.

This separation is important to assess how well the model generalizes to new, unseen data.

There are several commonly used techniques for model evaluation and validation, including the following:

a. Accuracy Metrics: Accuracy is a fundamental measure of a model's performance. It measures the proportion of correctly classified instances or the closeness of predicted values to actual values. Common accuracy metrics include accuracy rate, precision, recall, F1 score, and area under the receiver operating characteristic curve (AUC-ROC).

b. Cross-Validation: Cross-validation is a technique used to estimate the performance of a model when the data is limited. It involves partitioning the available data into multiple subsets, often referred to as "folds." The model is then trained on a subset of folds and tested on the remaining fold. This process is repeated multiple times, and the average performance across all folds is calculated.

c. Confusion Matrix: A confusion matrix provides a detailed breakdown of a model's performance by displaying the number of true positives, true negatives, false positives, and false negatives. It is particularly useful for evaluating classification models and determining their accuracy in predicting different classes.

d. Overfitting and Underfitting Analysis: Overfitting occurs when a model performs exceptionally well on the training data but fails to generalize to unseen data. Underfitting, on the other hand, happens when a model fails to capture the underlying patterns in the data. To address these issues, various techniques such as regularization and adjusting model complexity can be employed.

e. Validation Curves and Learning Curves: Validation curves and learning curves help assess the model's bias and variance. A validation curve measures the model's performance against different hyperparameters, allowing the selection of the optimal configuration. Learning curves show how the model's performance improves as the amount of training data increases, indicating whether more data is needed or if the model has reached its performance plateau.

f. Ensemble Methods: Ensemble methods combine multiple models to improve prediction accuracy. Techniques such as bagging (bootstrap aggregating), boosting, and stacking are used to create diverse models and aggregate their predictions.

Ensemble methods are effective in reducing overfitting and improving the overall performance of a model.

It is important to note that model evaluation and validation are iterative processes. They involve testing and refining the model multiple times to ensure its robustness and reliability. Additionally, the choice of evaluation techniques depends on the specific problem, the nature of the data, and the business requirements.

By thoroughly evaluating and validating models, businesses can make informed decisions based on reliable predictions and insights, leading to better outcomes and improved performance in various domains such as marketing, finance, operations, and customer analytics.

6.4 Feature Selection and Feature Engineering

Feature Selection:

Feature selection refers to the process of selecting a subset of relevant features (variables) from a larger set of available features. The goal is to identify the most informative and discriminative features that contribute significantly to the predictive performance of a model.

The importance of feature selection lies in its ability to enhance model accuracy, improve interpretability, reduce overfitting, and decrease computational complexity. By eliminating irrelevant or redundant features, we can focus on the most influential factors, which leads to more efficient and robust models.

There are several techniques for feature selection, including:

a. Univariate Selection: This approach evaluates each feature independently based on statistical tests and selects the features with the highest scores.

b. Recursive Feature Elimination (RFE): RFE starts with all features and progressively removes the least important ones by considering the model's performance after each elimination.

c. Principal Component Analysis (PCA): PCA transforms the original features into a new set of uncorrelated variables, called principal components. These components capture the maximum variance in the data and can be used as reduced features.

d. Regularization Methods: Techniques like Lasso and Ridge regression apply penalties to the model coefficients, encouraging sparsity and effectively performing feature selection.

Feature Engineering:

Feature engineering involves creating new features or transforming existing features to enhance the predictive power of a model. It focuses on extracting valuable information from the raw data and representing it in a more meaningful way for the machine learning algorithms.

Feature engineering can include the following techniques:

a. Encoding Categorical Variables: Categorical variables often require encoding to numerical representations that algorithms can process. Common methods include one-hot encoding, label encoding, and target encoding.

b. Handling Missing Values: Missing values can significantly impact model performance. Feature engineering techniques can involve imputing missing values using methods such as mean, median, or regression-based imputation.

c. Scaling and Normalization: Features with different scales can affect model performance. Scaling techniques like standardization (mean=0, variance=1) or normalization (rescaling to a specific range) can ensure features are on a similar scale.

d. Interaction and Polynomial Features: Creating interaction terms and polynomial features can capture complex relationships between variables that might not be apparent in their original form.

e. Time-based Features: For time-series data, deriving features such as lagged values, rolling averages, or trend indicators can capture temporal patterns and improve forecasting accuracy.

f. Domain-specific Knowledge: Incorporating domain expertise and understanding of the problem can help create features that are tailored to the specific context and improve model performance.

Overall, feature selection and feature engineering are vital steps in the data analysis pipeline. They contribute to building robust and accurate models by focusing on relevant features and transforming the data to better represent the underlying patterns. These techniques empower businesses to extract actionable insights, make informed decisions, and optimize their operations based on the outcomes of the analytics process.

CHAPTER 7

DATA VISUALIZATION AND REPORTING

7.1 Importance of Data Visualization

Data visualization refers to the representation of data in graphical or visual format, enabling businesses to understand and communicate insights effectively. Here are several key reasons why data visualization is crucial:

a. Enhances Data Understanding: Visualizing data helps individuals grasp complex information more easily. By presenting data visually through charts, graphs, or dashboards, patterns, trends, and relationships become apparent, allowing for a deeper understanding of the data. This enables stakeholders to make informed decisions and take appropriate actions.

b. Facilitates Decision-Making: Data visualization empowers decision-makers by providing clear and concise information. By visually presenting relevant data, businesses can quickly identify trends, outliers, and correlations, enabling them to make data-driven decisions swiftly. Visuals also support the communication of insights across teams and departments, fostering a shared understanding and alignment.

c. Increases Efficiency and Accuracy: Traditional data analysis methods often involve poring over spreadsheets and large datasets, which can be time-consuming and prone to errors. Data visualization streamlines this process by presenting data visually, enabling analysts to identify patterns and anomalies more efficiently. By reducing manual effort and potential mistakes, businesses can improve accuracy and save valuable time.

d. Supports Storytelling: Data visualization plays a significant role in storytelling, as it allows analysts to present data in a compelling and persuasive manner. By creating visually appealing and interactive visuals, complex information can be transformed into meaningful narratives. This enables stakeholders to absorb information more effectively and engage with the data, leading to better comprehension and retention.

e. Enhances Communication and Collaboration: Data visualization serves as a universal language that transcends technical barriers. Visual representations of data are easily understandable by both technical and non-technical stakeholders, facilitating effective communication and collaboration across teams. This fosters a data-driven culture within organizations and encourages data-driven decision-making at all levels.

f. Unveils Insights and Opportunities: Effective data visualization uncovers valuable insights and identifies new opportunities for businesses. By visualizing data, patterns and trends that might have otherwise gone unnoticed can be discovered. These insights can help organizations optimize operations, identify customer preferences, and drive innovation, leading to a competitive advantage in the market.

g. Improves Data Transparency: Data visualization promotes transparency within organizations by making data accessible and understandable to all stakeholders. By providing visual representations of data, businesses can ensure that relevant information is communicated transparently, fostering trust and credibility. This is particularly important in today's data-driven world, where transparency and accountability are highly valued.

Overall, data visualization is of paramount importance in business analytics. It enhances data understanding, facilitates decision-making, increases efficiency and accuracy, supports storytelling, enhances communication and collaboration, unveils insights and opportunities, and improves data transparency. By leveraging the power of visual representation, businesses can unlock the full potential of their data and gain a competitive edge in today's data-driven landscape.

7.2 Visualization Tools and Techniques

Visualization tools and techniques play a crucial role in business analytics by helping professionals effectively communicate insights and complex data to stakeholders. These tools enable users to transform raw data into meaningful visual representations, facilitating the understanding of patterns, trends, and relationships within the data. In this section, I will cover various aspects of visualization tools and techniques.

Importance of Visualization:

Visualization enhances data comprehension and aids in decision-making by presenting information in a visual format that is easy to understand and interpret. It allows users to identify patterns, outliers, and correlations quickly, leading to more informed insights and actions. Furthermore, visualizations facilitate the storytelling aspect of data analysis, enabling analysts to communicate findings in a compelling and persuasive manner.

Types of Visualizations:

There are several types of visualizations that serve different purposes based on the data and the insights sought. Common types include:

a. Bar Charts: Useful for comparing categorical data or displaying trends over time.

b. Line Charts: Ideal for showing continuous data trends and patterns over time.

c. Scatter Plots: Effective for exploring relationships and correlations between variables.

d. Pie Charts: Suitable for illustrating proportions and percentages of categorical data.

e. Heatmaps: Effective for displaying dense and multidimensional data through color gradients.

f. Treemaps: Useful for visualizing hierarchical data structures and comparing proportions.

g. Geographic Maps: Valuable for displaying spatial data and regional variations.

h. Gantt Charts: Ideal for project management, showcasing task timelines and dependencies.

Visualization Tools:

There are numerous visualization tools available, catering to different user needs and skill levels. Here are some popular tools:

a. Tableau: A widely used tool with a user-friendly interface, offering a broad range of visualization options.

b. Power BI: A Microsoft product that integrates well with other Microsoft tools, providing interactive and customizable visuals.

c. QlikView/Qlik Sense: Tools that offer powerful data exploration capabilities and self-service analytics.

d. Python Libraries: Matplotlib, Seaborn, and Plotly are popular libraries that provide flexibility and customization options for visualizations.

e. R: A programming language with libraries like ggplot2 and plotly, offering extensive visualization capabilities.

f. Google Data Studio: A free web-based tool that allows users to create interactive dashboards and reports.

Best Practices for Effective Visualization:

To create impactful visualizations, consider the following best practices:

a. Understand the audience: Tailor the visualizations to match the audience's knowledge level and objectives.

b. Keep it simple: Avoid clutter and focus on conveying the main message clearly.

c. Choose appropriate visuals: Select the most suitable chart types that effectively represent the data and insights.

d. Use color and formatting wisely: Leverage color to highlight key elements and maintain consistency throughout the visualizations.

e. Provide context: Include titles, labels, and annotations to provide clarity and aid interpretation.

f. Interactivity: Incorporate interactive features, such as filters and drill-down capabilities, to enable users to explore the data further.

g. Test and iterate: Review the visualizations with stakeholders and iterate based on feedback to ensure effectiveness.

Overall, visualization tools and techniques are essential for business analytics as they enable effective communication of insights. By choosing the right visualization types and leveraging suitable tools, professionals can transform complex data into meaningful and actionable visual representations that drive informed decision-making.

7.3 Dashboard Design and Reporting

Dashboard Design and Reporting play a crucial role in business analytics, providing a concise and visual representation of key metrics and insights. Effective dashboard design allows businesses to track and monitor performance, make data-driven decisions, and communicate information effectively to stakeholders. Here's an extensive explanation of dashboard design and reporting.

Dashboard Design:

a. Purpose and Audience: Clearly define the purpose of the dashboard and identify the target audience. Understand the specific questions or decisions the dashboard needs to address and the information relevant to the audience.

b. Key Performance Indicators (KPIs): Determine the critical metrics that align with business goals and measure performance. Focus on a limited set of KPIs to avoid clutter and ensure clarity. Examples include sales revenue, customer satisfaction score, conversion rates, or website traffic.

c. Data Sources and Integration: Identify the data sources required to populate the dashboard. This can include databases, spreadsheets, APIs, or other systems. Ensure the data is clean, accurate, and integrated into a single source for consistency.

d. Visualization Techniques: Choose appropriate visualizations to represent data effectively. Use charts (e.g., line charts, bar charts, pie charts), graphs, tables, and gauges that best convey the insights and facilitate quick understanding. Avoid unnecessary decorations and excessive colors that may distract from the data.

e. Layout and Structure: Organize the dashboard in a logical and intuitive manner. Place the most critical information prominently, allowing users to grasp key insights at a glance. Group related information together and use clear headings, labels, and legends to guide interpretation.

f. Interactivity and Filters: Incorporate interactive elements such as filters, dropdowns, or drill-down options. This empowers users to explore data in more detail, customize views, and extract specific insights based on their needs. However, ensure interactivity doesn't overwhelm or confuse users.

g. Responsiveness and Compatibility: Design dashboards that are responsive and compatible with different devices and screen sizes. Ensure the layout and visualizations adapt well to desktops, tablets, and mobile devices, enabling users to access and view the dashboards conveniently.

Reporting:

a. Report Types: Understand the different types of reports required, such as operational reports, executive summaries, ad-hoc reports, or periodic performance reports. Each report type serves a specific purpose and audience, influencing the content and format.

b. Report Structure: Develop a consistent and logical structure for reports. Typically, reports include a title, executive summary, methodology, findings, analysis, recommendations, and appendices. Present information in a logical flow to facilitate easy comprehension.

c. Data Visualization: Incorporate visual elements such as charts, graphs, and tables to present data in a visually appealing and accessible manner. Use appropriate visuals to support the narrative and highlight key findings effectively.

d. Clear and Concise Writing: Use clear and concise language in reporting, avoiding jargon and unnecessary complexity. Ensure the content is easily understandable by the target audience. Use headings, bullet points, and subheadings to enhance readability.

e. Actionable Insights: Provide meaningful insights and actionable recommendations based on the data analysis. Clearly outline the implications of the findings and suggest concrete steps that can be taken to improve performance or address challenges.

f. Timeliness and Frequency: Determine the appropriate frequency of reporting based on the needs of the audience. Some reports may be required daily, while others may be monthly or quarterly. Deliver reports in a timely manner to ensure the information is relevant and up to date.

g. Distribution and Accessibility: Choose the appropriate channels and platforms for distributing reports. This can include email, shared drives, collaboration tools, or dedicated reporting platforms. Ensure that the reports are easily accessible to the intended recipients and maintain proper security measures for sensitive information.

By following these guidelines, businesses can create well-designed dashboards and reports that effectively communicate key information and insights.

Here are additional points to consider:

Dashboard Design (continued):

Color and Typography: Use a cohesive color scheme that aligns with the organization's branding and ensures visual harmony. Choose appropriate font sizes, styles, and colors for text elements to enhance readability. Maintain consistency throughout the dashboard.

Real-Time Data and Automation: Whenever possible, integrate real-time data feeds into the dashboard to provide up-to-the-minute information. Automate data updates and refreshes to ensure accuracy and save time. This allows users to monitor live performance and respond quickly to changes.

Storytelling and Narrative: Design dashboards that tell a compelling story and guide users through the data. Use annotations, captions, or commentary to provide context and highlight key insights. Present data in a logical sequence that facilitates understanding and decision-making.

Reporting (continued):

Visual Hierarchy: Use a clear visual hierarchy in reports to guide readers' attention. Use headings, subheadings, bullet points, and numbering to structure the content. Emphasize important findings and recommendations through formatting techniques like bolding or color highlighting.

Data Accuracy and Verification: Ensure data accuracy and conduct thorough verification before including it in reports. Use reliable sources, cross-check information, and validate calculations to maintain credibility. Clearly state the data sources and methodologies used to build trust with readers.

Iterative Improvement: Continuously gather feedback from report recipients and stakeholders to improve the reporting process. Seek input on the relevance, clarity, and usefulness of the reports. Incorporate suggestions and make necessary adjustments to enhance the reporting experience.

Data Security and Privacy: Pay attention to data security and privacy regulations when handling sensitive information in reports. Ensure that appropriate measures are in place to protect data, comply with regulations, and obtain necessary permissions for data sharing.

Training and Support: Provide training and support to users of dashboards and reports. Offer guidance on interpreting the data, understanding visualizations, and leveraging the insights for decision-making. Address any questions or concerns raised by users promptly and effectively.

Overall, effective dashboard design and reporting are essential components of business analytics. They enable organizations to monitor performance, gain insights, and communicate information in a concise and visually appealing manner. By considering the purpose, audience, data integration, visualization techniques, and interactivity, you can design informative and user-friendly dashboards. Similarly, structuring reports, incorporating visualizations, ensuring clarity, and providing actionable insights contribute to the effectiveness of reporting. Continuous improvement, data accuracy, and adherence to security and privacy standards further enhance the impact of dashboards and reports in supporting data-driven decision-making.

CHAPTER 8

BUSINESS INTELLIGENCE AND DECISION SUPPORT SYSTEMS

8.1 Business Intelligence (BI) Overview

Business Intelligence (BI) is a comprehensive approach to gathering, analyzing, and visualizing data within an organization to drive informed decision-making. It involves the use of various technologies, processes, and applications to transform raw data into meaningful insights and actionable information.

BI provides a holistic view of an organization's data by integrating data from different sources such as databases, spreadsheets, and enterprise systems. These sources can include customer data, sales data, financial data, operational data, and more. By consolidating and organizing this data, BI allows businesses to gain a better understanding of their operations, identify trends, and make data-driven decisions.

One of the key components of BI is data integration, which involves extracting data from multiple sources and transforming it into a unified format. This integration process ensures data consistency and accuracy, enabling analysts and decision-makers to work with reliable and up-to-date information.

Once the data is integrated, the next step is data analysis. BI tools and techniques enable analysts to perform various types of analysis, such as descriptive, diagnostic, predictive, and prescriptive analysis. Descriptive analysis helps to summarize and present historical data, while diagnostic analysis investigates the causes of past events. Predictive analysis uses statistical models and algorithms to forecast future trends, and prescriptive analysis suggests optimal courses of action based on the insights gained.

Visualization plays a crucial role in BI as it helps stakeholders comprehend complex data more easily. Dashboards, charts, graphs, and interactive reports are commonly used to present data in a visually appealing and intuitive manner. Visualizations enable users to identify patterns, spot anomalies, and uncover hidden relationships within the data, facilitating effective decision-making.

BI is not limited to historical or current data analysis; it also focuses on real-time or near-real-time data processing. This allows businesses to monitor key performance indicators (KPIs) and critical metrics in real-time, enabling timely interventions and adjustments to optimize business operations.

Moreover, BI supports a wide range of business functions, including finance, sales, marketing, supply chain management, and human resources. It empowers decision-makers at all levels of the organization to access relevant information and gain insights tailored to their specific roles and responsibilities.

The benefits of implementing BI in an organization are numerous. It enhances data-driven decision-making by providing accurate and timely information. BI enables businesses to identify opportunities, minimize risks, and optimize operational efficiency. It also enables proactive monitoring and tracking of performance metrics, fostering a culture of continuous improvement.

Overall, Business Intelligence is a powerful approach that combines technology, processes, and analytics to transform raw data into valuable insights. It enables businesses to make informed decisions, gain a competitive edge, and drive growth and success.

8.2 Components of BI Systems

Business Intelligence (BI) systems consist of several key components that work together to help organizations collect, analyze, and visualize data to support decision-making processes. These components include:

a. Data Sources: BI systems rely on various data sources, both internal and external, to gather relevant information. Internal data sources can include databases, data warehouses, and operational systems, while external sources may include market research reports, social media feeds, and public datasets. The quality and availability of data directly impact the effectiveness of the BI system.

b. Data Integration: Data integration is the process of combining data from multiple sources and transforming it into a unified format suitable for analysis. This component ensures that data from different systems or databases can be seamlessly merged and used for reporting and analysis. Data integration may involve tasks such as data cleansing, data transformation, and data enrichment.

c. Data Warehousing: A data warehouse is a centralized repository that stores large amounts of structured and sometimes semi-structured data collected from various sources. It is designed to support efficient querying, reporting, and analysis. Data warehouses often use a dimensional model that organizes data into facts (numeric measurements) and dimensions (descriptive attributes) to facilitate multidimensional analysis.

d. ETL (Extract, Transform, Load): ETL processes are used to extract data from source systems, transform it into a suitable format, and load it into the data warehouse. Extract involves retrieving data from different sources, transform includes cleaning, filtering, and aggregating the data, and load refers to the process of inserting the transformed data into the data warehouse.

e. Data Modeling: Data modeling involves designing the structure and relationships of the data stored in the data warehouse. It defines how data will be organized and represented to support efficient querying and analysis. Common data modeling techniques include entity-relationship diagrams (ERDs) and dimensional modeling, which create a logical and intuitive representation of the data.

f. Reporting and Visualization: The reporting and visualization component enables users to analyze and interpret data through visually appealing dashboards, charts, and graphs. It allows users to gain insights and identify trends, patterns, and anomalies in the data.

Reporting and visualization tools often provide interactive capabilities, allowing users to explore data and drill down into specific details.

g. Analytics and Business Intelligence Tools: These tools provide advanced analytical capabilities, such as data mining, predictive modeling, and statistical analysis. They enable users to uncover hidden patterns, perform complex calculations, and generate forecasts. Business intelligence tools also support ad hoc querying and self-service analytics, empowering users to explore data and create customized reports without extensive technical knowledge.

h. Data Governance: Data governance ensures the availability, integrity, and security of data within the BI system. It involves establishing policies, procedures, and controls to manage data quality, metadata management, data privacy, and compliance. Effective data governance promotes trust in the data and ensures that it is accurate, consistent, and reliable for decision-making.

i. User Interface and Collaboration: The user interface component focuses on providing an intuitive and user-friendly interface for interacting with the BI system. It enables users to access reports, dashboards, and analytics tools, and supports collaboration by allowing users to share insights, annotate data, and collaborate on analysis projects. User-friendly interfaces enhance user adoption and engagement with the BI system.

j. Performance Management: Performance management components enable organizations to monitor and track key performance indicators (KPIs) and align them with strategic goals. They facilitate the measurement of performance, the identification of areas for improvement, and the monitoring of progress towards objectives. Performance management features often include scorecards, alerts, and exception reporting.

These components work together to create a comprehensive BI system that enables organizations to leverage data-driven insights for better decision-making, improved operational efficiency, and competitive advantage. Each component plays a crucial role in the success and effectiveness of a BI system. The integration of these components allows organizations to transform raw data into valuable insights and actionable information. By leveraging BI systems, businesses can make informed decisions, identify trends and patterns, optimize processes, and gain a competitive edge in the market.

8.3 Decision Support Systems (DSS)

Decision Support Systems (DSS) are computer-based tools or software applications that assist businesses in making informed and effective decisions. They are designed to provide managers and decision-makers with the necessary information and analytical capabilities to solve complex problems and support decision-making processes.

DSS integrates various data sources, models, and analytical techniques to help users analyze information, evaluate alternatives, and make decisions based on a structured approach. Here are some key aspects of Decision Support Systems:

a. Data Management: DSS relies on data from different sources, such as databases, spreadsheets, and external sources. It includes data extraction, cleaning, transformation, and storage processes to ensure data accuracy and availability for analysis.

b. Modeling and Analysis: DSS employs mathematical and statistical models to represent real-world situations and simulate different scenarios. These models allow decision-makers to evaluate the potential outcomes of different decisions and understand the impact of various variables on the decision-making process.

c. What-If Analysis: DSS facilitates "what-if" analysis, enabling users to manipulate variables and assess the potential outcomes of different scenarios. By changing inputs and assumptions, decision-makers can explore alternative options and understand the implications of their decisions before implementation.

d. Decision Optimization: DSS incorporates optimization techniques to identify the best possible solution among a set of alternatives. These techniques consider multiple objectives, constraints, and preferences to help decision-makers find an optimal or near-optimal solution that aligns with their goals.

e. Data Visualization: DSS often includes data visualization tools that present information in a visually appealing and intuitive manner. Graphs, charts, and interactive dashboards help decision-makers understand complex data patterns, trends, and relationships quickly, facilitating effective decision-making.

f. Collaboration and Communication: DSS supports collaboration among decision-makers by providing a platform to share information, insights, and analysis. It allows multiple stakeholders to contribute their expertise, review recommendations, and collectively make informed decisions.

g. Real-Time Decision Support: Some advanced DSS solutions leverage real-time data integration and analytics capabilities. They provide decision-makers with up-to-date information and insights, enabling them to respond promptly to dynamic market conditions and make agile decisions.

h. Integration with Existing Systems: DSS can integrate with existing business systems, such as enterprise resource planning (ERP) or customer relationship management (CRM) systems. This integration enables decision-makers to leverage data from various sources and obtain a comprehensive view of the organization's operations and performance.

i. Decision Support for Different Levels: DSS caters to the needs of various levels within an organization, including strategic, tactical, and operational decision-making. Strategic DSS assists top-level executives in long-term planning and strategic initiatives, while tactical and operational DSS focus on day-to-day decision-making and performance monitoring.

Overall, Decision Support Systems (DSS) are computer-based tools that combine data management, modeling, analysis, visualization, and collaboration capabilities to support decision-making processes. By leveraging these systems, organizations can enhance the quality and effectiveness of their decisions, leading to improved performance and competitive advantage.

8.4 Implementing BI and DSS in Organizations

Implementing Business Intelligence (BI) and Decision Support Systems (DSS) in organizations can significantly enhance their ability to make data-driven decisions and gain valuable insights. Let's dive into the details of these implementations.

Business Intelligence (BI):

BI refers to the technologies, processes, and practices used to collect, integrate, analyze, and present business information. The goal of BI is to provide actionable insights and support decision-making at various levels within an organization.

a. Identify Business Objectives: Before implementing BI, it's crucial to understand the organization's business objectives and the specific problems it aims to solve. This helps in aligning the BI implementation with the strategic goals of the organization.

b. Data Gathering and Integration: The first step in implementing BI is to gather relevant data from various sources within the organization. This data could include transactional records, customer data, sales data, and more. Integrating data from different sources ensures a unified view and helps uncover hidden relationships and patterns.

c. Data Warehousing: To facilitate efficient analysis, the gathered data needs to be stored in a central repository called a data warehouse. A data warehouse provides a structured and optimized environment for storing and managing large volumes of data. It also enables historical data analysis and supports complex queries.

d. Data Modeling and ETL: Extract, Transform, Load (ETL) processes are used to cleanse, transform, and load data into the data warehouse. Data modeling techniques, such as dimensional modeling, are applied to structure the data for efficient analysis. This step involves designing fact tables, dimension tables, and establishing relationships between them.

e. Reporting and Visualization: Once the data is ready, BI tools are employed to create reports, dashboards, and visualizations that present the analyzed information in a user-friendly manner. These visual representations make it easier for decision-makers to interpret the data, identify trends, and gain insights.

Decision Support Systems (DSS):

DSS are interactive computer-based systems designed to assist decision-makers in solving complex problems. These systems leverage data, models, and analytical techniques to support decision-making processes.

a. Problem Definition: The first step in implementing a DSS is to clearly define the problem or decision that needs to be addressed. This involves understanding the decision context, identifying decision criteria, and specifying the desired outcomes.

b. Data Gathering and Analysis: Relevant data is collected from internal and external sources. Analytical techniques, such as statistical analysis, data mining, or predictive modeling, are applied to gain insights from the data. These techniques can help in identifying patterns, predicting future outcomes, and evaluating various decision alternatives.

c. Model Development: Decision models are created based on the identified problem and decision criteria. These models can be mathematical, simulation-based, or rule-based, depending on the nature of the problem. The models help simulate different scenarios and evaluate the potential outcomes of each decision alternative.

d. User Interface and Interactivity: DSS typically have user-friendly interfaces that allow decision-makers to interact with the system, input parameters, and explore different scenarios. The system provides real-time feedback, enabling users to assess the impact of their decisions and make informed choices.

e. Decision Implementation: Once a decision is made using the DSS, it needs to be implemented in the organization. This involves communicating the decision to relevant stakeholders, allocating resources, and monitoring the outcomes. DSS can also provide feedback mechanisms to evaluate the effectiveness of the decision and support continuous improvement.

Overall, implementing BI and DSS in organizations involves understanding business objectives, gathering and integrating data, building data warehouses, analyzing data, creating reports and visualizations for BI, defining problems, gathering and analyzing data, developing decision models, and providing user-friendly interfaces for DSS. These implementations empower organizations to harness the power of data and make more informed and effective decisions.

CHAPTER 9

ETHICAL AND LEGAL CONSIDERATIONS IN BUSINESS ANALYTICS

9.1 Ethical Issues in Business Analytics

Ethical issues in business analytics refer to the moral dilemmas and concerns that arise when applying analytical techniques and technologies to gather, analyze, and interpret data in a business context. Business analytics involves extracting insights from data to inform decision-making, optimize processes, and gain a competitive advantage. However, the use of data analytics also raises ethical considerations that must be addressed to ensure responsible and fair practices.

a. Privacy and data protection: One of the key ethical concerns in business analytics is the protection of individual privacy. Organizations must obtain informed consent from individuals when collecting their data, and they should handle and store that data securely. Additionally, organizations should clearly communicate how data will be used and ensure that it is used only for the intended purposes. Anonymization and data aggregation techniques can help protect individual identities while still extracting valuable insights.

b. Fairness and bias: Business analytics can inadvertently perpetuate bias if not implemented carefully. Bias can occur in various stages of the analytics process, such as data collection, data preprocessing, algorithm development, and decision-making based on the analytics results. Bias can result from historical inequalities, incomplete or unrepresentative data, or algorithmic biases. It is crucial to assess and mitigate bias to ensure fair treatment of individuals and avoid discriminatory practices.

c. Transparency and explainability: The increasing complexity of analytics techniques, such as machine learning and artificial intelligence, can make it challenging to understand and interpret the decisions made by algorithms. It is important to ensure transparency and explainability in analytics models and their outcomes. Organizations should strive to provide clear explanations of how decisions are made, especially when they impact individuals or have significant consequences.

d. Accountability and responsibility: Organizations using business analytics should be accountable for the decisions and actions they take based on analytics insights. Accountability involves taking responsibility for the potential consequences of using analytics, including unintended negative outcomes. Organizations should establish guidelines, policies, and governance frameworks to ensure ethical practices in analytics and should have mechanisms in place to address concerns and complaints from individuals affected by analytics processes.

e. Intellectual property and data ownership: Data collected and used in business analytics often raises questions about ownership and intellectual property rights. Organizations should ensure they have appropriate permissions and legal rights to use the data. Additionally, they should respect intellectual property rights when using third-party data sources, ensuring compliance with licensing agreements and copyright laws.

f. Social implications: Business analytics can have broader societal impacts, and organizations should consider the potential social consequences of their analytics practices. For example, automated decision-making systems can influence access to opportunities, resource allocation, and social dynamics. It is essential to assess and mitigate any potential negative impacts to ensure the ethical use of analytics and promote social good.

To address these ethical issues, organizations should establish clear ethical guidelines and policies for business analytics. They should prioritize the responsible use of data, ensure transparency in their analytics processes, conduct regular audits to identify and mitigate biases, and provide mechanisms for individuals to exercise their rights and voice concerns. Collaboration with ethicists, legal experts, and diverse stakeholders can help organizations navigate the ethical challenges associated with business analytics.

9.2 Privacy and Data Protection

Privacy and data protection are crucial aspects of modern business analytics. They refer to the measures and regulations put in place to safeguard individuals' personal information and ensure its responsible handling and storage. Let's delve into the topic more extensively.

Privacy refers to an individual's right to control the collection, use, and disclosure of their personal information. It encompasses the protection of sensitive data, such as names, addresses, phone numbers, social security numbers, financial records, and any other personally identifiable information (PII). Maintaining privacy is essential as it ensures that individuals have the power to decide how their data is used and who has access to it.

Data protection, on the other hand, focuses on safeguarding data from unauthorized access, alteration, or destruction. It encompasses various technical, organizational, and legal measures implemented to ensure the confidentiality, integrity, and availability of data. Data protection measures involve encryption, access controls, secure storage, regular backups, and monitoring for potential breaches or vulnerabilities.

In the context of business analytics, privacy and data protection play crucial roles in establishing trust with customers and stakeholders. When organizations collect and analyze data, they must be transparent about the purpose and scope of data collection, ensure the data's accuracy, and obtain appropriate consent from individuals. An ethical approach to business analytics involves respecting privacy rights and adhering to relevant privacy laws and regulations.

Privacy regulations, such as the General Data Protection Regulation (GDPR) in Europe or the California Consumer Privacy Act (CCPA) in the United States, impose legal obligations on businesses regarding data protection and individual privacy. These regulations require organizations to obtain consent before collecting and using personal data, provide individuals with access to their data, allow them to correct or delete their data, and implement measures to protect data from breaches.

To comply with privacy and data protection regulations, businesses must adopt a privacy-by-design approach. This means integrating privacy considerations into every stage of data collection, processing, and storage. It involves implementing privacy policies, conducting privacy impact assessments, and regularly auditing data handling practices to ensure compliance. Additionally, organizations must educate their employees on privacy best practices and establish protocols for data breach response and notification.

You have a responsibility to ensure that data analytics initiatives are conducted ethically and in compliance with privacy and data protection regulations. You must understand the legal requirements, assess the risks associated with data processing, and implement appropriate technical and organizational measures to protect personal information.

Overall, privacy and data protection are critical aspects of business analytics. They involve respecting individuals' rights to control their personal information and implementing measures to safeguard data from unauthorized access or misuse. By adhering to privacy regulations, adopting privacy-by-design principles, and prioritizing data security, businesses can build trust with their customers while harnessing the power of data for valuable insights and informed decision-making.

9.3 Regulatory Compliance

Regulatory compliance refers to the adherence to laws, regulations, guidelines, and standards that are set by governing bodies within a particular industry or jurisdiction. It is a crucial aspect of business operations as it ensures that companies operate within the legal framework and meet the requirements established to protect consumers, maintain fair competition, and uphold public safety.

In today's business landscape, regulatory compliance has become increasingly complex and demanding due to the ever-changing nature of laws and regulations. Businesses are subject to a wide range of compliance obligations, including data privacy, consumer protection, environmental regulations, financial reporting, occupational health and safety, and many more, depending on their industry and geographical location.

Here are some key aspects to consider when addressing regulatory compliance:

a. Understanding Regulations: It is crucial to have a comprehensive understanding of relevant laws and regulations applicable to the industry in which the business operates. This requires ongoing monitoring of regulatory updates and staying informed about changes that may affect the organization.

b. Assessing Compliance Risks: Conducting a thorough risk assessment is vital to identify potential compliance gaps and vulnerabilities within the organization. This involves evaluating the likelihood and impact of non-compliance, considering both legal consequences and reputational risks.

c. Developing Compliance Programs: Based on the identified risks, developing and implementing robust compliance programs is essential. These programs typically include policies, procedures, and controls to ensure adherence to regulations, as well as training programs to educate employees on compliance requirements.

d. Data Analysis and Monitoring: Utilizing data analytics tools and techniques can help identify patterns, anomalies, and potential compliance issues. By analyzing relevant data, such as financial transactions, customer interactions, or operational metrics, businesses can proactively detect any deviations from regulatory requirements and take corrective action promptly.

e. Reporting and Documentation: Maintaining accurate and up-to-date documentation is crucial for demonstrating compliance to regulatory authorities. This includes record-keeping, documenting policies and procedures, and preparing reports required by regulatory bodies.

f. Audits and Assessments: Conducting regular internal audits and assessments can help evaluate the effectiveness of compliance programs, identify areas for improvement, and ensure ongoing adherence to regulations. External audits by independent parties may also be necessary in some cases.

g. Embracing Technology Solutions: Leveraging technology, such as compliance management software or automation tools, can streamline compliance processes, enhance efficiency, and provide real-time monitoring of compliance activities.

h. Continuous Monitoring and Adaptation: Regulatory landscapes are subject to frequent changes. Therefore, continuous monitoring of regulatory developments and proactive adaptation of compliance strategies are essential to stay ahead of evolving requirements.

Failure to comply with regulatory obligations can have severe consequences for businesses, including financial penalties, legal actions, damage to reputation, and even the suspension of operations. Therefore, your role would involve assisting organizations in effectively managing regulatory compliance through data-driven insights, risk assessments, process optimizations, and the implementation of robust compliance programs.

CHAPTER 10

CASE STUDIES AND PRACTICAL APPLICATIONS

10.1 Real-World Business Analytics Use Cases

Business analytics encompasses the use of data and statistical techniques to gain insights, make informed decisions, and drive improvements in various aspects of an organization's operations. Here are some prominent use cases:

a. Customer Analytics: Organizations use customer analytics to understand their customers better, predict their behavior, and enhance customer satisfaction. This includes segmentation, where customers are grouped based on characteristics such as demographics, buying patterns, or preferences. By analyzing customer data, businesses can personalize marketing efforts, optimize product offerings, and improve customer retention.

b. Sales and Revenue Optimization: Business analytics helps optimize sales and revenue by analyzing historical sales data, market trends, and customer behavior. This enables organizations to identify cross-selling and upselling opportunities, forecast demand, determine optimal pricing strategies, and allocate resources effectively. By leveraging predictive analytics models, companies can enhance sales performance and maximize revenue.

c. Supply Chain Analytics: Supply chain analytics enables organizations to optimize their supply chain processes, reduce costs, and improve operational efficiency. By analyzing data related to inventory levels, transportation, lead times, and supplier performance, businesses can identify bottlenecks, optimize inventory levels, and enhance supply chain responsiveness. Predictive analytics can also be used to anticipate demand fluctuations and mitigate supply chain disruptions.

d. Financial Analytics: Financial analytics involves the analysis of financial data to gain insights into an organization's financial performance, profitability, and risk exposure. It includes financial forecasting, budgeting, and variance analysis to support strategic decision-making. By leveraging financial analytics, companies can identify cost-saving opportunities, optimize resource allocation, and assess the financial viability of projects or investments.

e. Fraud Detection and Risk Management: Business analytics plays a crucial role in identifying and mitigating risks, including fraud. By analyzing large volumes of transactional data, organizations can detect anomalies and patterns indicative of fraudulent activities. Advanced analytics techniques, such as machine learning algorithms, enable the development of predictive models that can identify potential fraud cases in real-time, minimizing financial losses and reputational damage.

f. Marketing Analytics: Marketing analytics helps organizations measure the effectiveness of marketing campaigns, optimize marketing spend, and improve customer acquisition. It involves analyzing data from various marketing channels, such as digital advertising, social media, and email marketing. By measuring key performance indicators (KPIs) such as conversion rates, customer engagement, and return on investment (ROI), businesses can fine-tune their marketing strategies and improve overall marketing effectiveness.

g. Operational Analytics: Operational analytics focuses on improving operational efficiency and performance across different functional areas of an organization. It involves analyzing data from production processes, logistics, quality control, and resource utilization. By identifying inefficiencies, process bottlenecks, and areas of improvement, companies can optimize operations, reduce costs, and enhance productivity.

h. Churn Prediction and Customer Retention: Analytics can help businesses identify customers at risk of churn (leaving) by analyzing historical data and customer behavior patterns. By predicting churn, businesses can take proactive measures to retain customers, such as targeted retention campaigns, personalized offers, and improved customer service, ultimately reducing customer attrition and increasing customer lifetime value.

i. HR Analytics: HR analytics leverages data to optimize human resources management processes. It includes analyzing employee data to identify patterns related to employee performance, engagement, retention, and recruitment. By utilizing HR analytics, organizations can make data-driven decisions regarding talent acquisition, performance management, employee development, and workforce planning.

These are just a few examples of real-world business analytics use cases. The application of analytics extends across various industries and functional areas, enabling organizations to gain insights, improve decision-making, optimize processes, improve profitability, and achieve competitive advantage in today's data-driven business landscape.

10.2 Application of Business Analytics in Various Industries

Business analytics plays a crucial role in various industries by enabling organizations to make data-driven decisions and gain valuable insights. Here are some examples of how business analytics is applied in different sectors:

a. Retail Industry: Retailers leverage business analytics to analyze customer behavior, optimize pricing strategies, and manage inventory. They use data to identify customer preferences, anticipate demand patterns, and personalize marketing campaigns. Additionally, retailers use analytics to optimize store layouts and improve supply chain efficiency.

b. Finance and Banking: In the finance industry, business analytics helps banks and financial institutions manage risk, detect fraud, and improve customer satisfaction. Analytics is used to assess creditworthiness, identify potentially fraudulent activities, and develop personalized financial products based on customer needs. It also plays a role in portfolio management, predicting market trends, and optimizing investment strategies.

c. Healthcare Industry: Business analytics is transforming healthcare by improving patient outcomes, optimizing resource allocation, and enhancing operational efficiency. Analytics enables healthcare providers to analyze patient data, identify disease patterns, and develop predictive models for early detection and intervention. It also helps hospitals in managing resources effectively, reducing costs, and improving patient satisfaction.

d. Manufacturing and Supply Chain: Analytics is widely used in manufacturing and supply chain management to optimize production processes, manage inventory levels, and improve logistics. By analyzing historical and real-time data, manufacturers can identify bottlenecks, optimize production schedules, and reduce downtime. Supply chain analytics helps in demand forecasting, supplier management, and optimizing transportation routes.

e. Telecommunications: Telecom companies utilize business analytics to improve customer experience, optimize network performance, and develop targeted marketing strategies. Analytics helps in predicting customer churn, analyzing call data records, and identifying network issues in real-time. Telecom providers also use analytics to offer personalized services and develop pricing plans based on customer usage patterns.

f. E-commerce: Business analytics plays a vital role in the e-commerce industry by analyzing customer behavior, optimizing product recommendations, and streamlining operations. E-commerce companies use analytics to track website traffic, analyze customer browsing and purchase history, and personalize product offerings. Additionally, analytics helps in optimizing supply chain operations, inventory management, and pricing strategies.

g. Energy and Utilities: Business analytics is used in the energy and utilities sector to optimize energy generation, monitor consumption patterns, and improve sustainability. Analytics helps in forecasting energy demand, optimizing power plant operations, and identifying energy-saving opportunities. It also aids in the integration of renewable energy sources, managing smart grids, and reducing carbon emissions.

h. Marketing and Advertising: Analytics plays a crucial role in marketing and advertising by providing insights into customer behavior, measuring campaign effectiveness, and optimizing marketing spend. Marketers use analytics to segment customers, identify target audiences, and personalize marketing messages. It also helps in measuring the return on investment (ROI) of marketing campaigns and optimizing advertising channels.

These are just a few examples of how business analytics is applied across different industries. The widespread use of analytics enables organizations to gain a competitive edge, improve decision-making, and drive business growth.

10.3 Successful Business Analytics Implementations

Successful business analytics implementations are critical for organizations looking to gain insights, make informed decisions, and drive positive outcomes. To ensure a successful implementation, several key factors should be considered and carefully addressed.

a. Clearly define goals and objectives: Start by clearly articulating the goals and objectives of the business analytics initiative. This involves identifying specific problems or opportunities that analytics can address and defining measurable outcomes that align with the organization's overall strategy.

b. Develop a robust data strategy: A strong data strategy is essential for successful analytics implementations. This involves assessing the organization's data landscape, identifying relevant data sources, ensuring data quality and integrity, and establishing processes for data collection, storage, and governance.

c. Select the right tools and technologies: Choosing the right analytics tools and technologies is crucial. Consider factors such as the organization's needs, scalability, ease of use, integration capabilities, and vendor support. Common tools include data visualization platforms, statistical software, machine learning frameworks, and cloud-based analytics platforms.

d. Build a skilled analytics team: A skilled and diverse analytics team is critical to the success of any implementation. This includes data scientists, business analysts, statisticians, and data engineers who possess the necessary technical skills and domain expertise. Investing in training and professional development can help build a competent team.

e. Foster a data-driven culture: To drive adoption and maximize the value of analytics, it is important to foster a data-driven culture within the organization. This involves promoting data literacy, encouraging data-driven decision-making, and creating a supportive environment where employees are empowered to leverage analytics for their work.

f. Collaborate across departments: Successful implementations require collaboration and alignment across different departments and functions. Business analytics should not be seen as a standalone initiative but as an integral part of the organization's overall strategy. Engage stakeholders from various areas to ensure their requirements are considered and addressed.

g. Start with small, focused projects: It is often beneficial to start with small, focused analytics projects that deliver quick wins and demonstrate the value of the initiative. These projects can help build momentum, gain stakeholder buy-in, and generate valuable insights that can drive further analytics initiatives.

h. Monitor and evaluate performance: Implementing analytics is an iterative process, and it is crucial to continuously monitor and evaluate the performance of the analytics solution. Establish key performance indicators (KPIs) and regularly track progress towards goals. Use feedback and insights gained from the analytics to refine and improve the implementation over time.

i. Scale and expand strategically: Once initial successes are achieved, it is important to scale and expand the analytics implementation strategically. This may involve integrating analytics into existing systems, expanding data sources, and extending the use of analytics across different areas of the organization. Develop a roadmap that outlines the incremental steps to expand the analytics capabilities effectively.

j. Stay updated and adapt: Business analytics is a rapidly evolving field, and it is crucial to stay updated with the latest trends, technologies, and best practices. Embrace a culture of continuous learning and improvement, and be willing to adapt the implementation strategy as needed to address changing business needs and technological advancements.

By considering these factors and following best practices, organizations can increase their chances of successful business analytics implementations, leading to data-driven insights, informed decision-making, and improved business outcomes.

CHAPTER 11: CONCLUSION

Business analytics involves using data to gain insights and make informed decisions. Key concepts include data collection, descriptive analytics (examining historical data), predictive analytics (forecasting future outcomes), prescriptive analytics (providing recommendations), data visualization (presenting data visually), data mining (finding patterns), machine learning (automating processes), KPIs (measuring performance), and data-driven decision making. By leveraging these concepts, businesses can optimize operations and achieve strategic objectives.

Future Trends in Business Analytics

Artificial Intelligence and Machine Learning: AI and ML technologies will continue to play a significant role in the future of business analytics. These technologies enable businesses to analyze vast amounts of data quickly and accurately, uncover patterns and insights, and make data-driven decisions. AI and ML algorithms can automate data processing, predictive modeling, and anomaly detection, enhancing the efficiency and effectiveness of business analytics.

a. Advanced Data Visualization: The demand for advanced data visualization tools will increase in the future. As data becomes more complex and diverse, businesses will seek interactive and intuitive visualization techniques to understand and communicate insights effectively. Advanced visualization techniques, such as interactive dashboards, augmented reality (AR), and virtual reality (VR) visualizations, will enable users to explore data and gain deeper insights.

b. Predictive and Prescriptive Analytics: While descriptive analytics focuses on understanding past events and current situations, predictive and prescriptive analytics will gain prominence. Predictive analytics leverages historical data and statistical techniques to forecast future outcomes, enabling businesses to make proactive decisions. Prescriptive analytics goes a step further by recommending actions to optimize business processes, improve performance, and achieve desired outcomes.

c. Real-time Analytics: The ability to process and analyze data in real-time will become increasingly important for businesses. Real-time analytics enables organizations to monitor and react to events as they happen, leading to timely decision-making and improved operational efficiency. With the advancement of technologies like in-memory computing and streaming analytics, businesses can gain instant insights from high-velocity data streams.

d. Privacy and Ethical Considerations: As data collection and analytics continue to expand, privacy and ethical concerns will become critical. Businesses will need to navigate the complexities of data privacy regulations, such as the General Data Protection Regulation (GDPR) and similar laws, to ensure responsible data usage. Ethical considerations, such as the fair use of data, avoiding bias, and maintaining transparency, will be essential for building trust with customers and stakeholders.

e. Natural Language Processing and Conversational Analytics: Natural Language Processing (NLP) and conversational analytics will play a significant role in the future of business analytics.

NLP techniques allow businesses to extract insights from unstructured data sources, such as customer reviews, social media posts, and support tickets. Conversational analytics, powered by technologies like chatbots and voice assistants, enables businesses to analyze and respond to customer queries and feedback in real-time.

f. Augmented Analytics: Augmented analytics combines machine learning and natural language processing to automate data preparation, insights generation, and visualization. These technologies enable business users with limited technical skills to perform sophisticated analytics tasks. Augmented analytics platforms offer automated recommendations, intelligent data exploration, and interactive dashboards, empowering users to make data-driven decisions without extensive knowledge of data science.

g. Edge Analytics: The proliferation of Internet of Things (IoT) devices and edge computing will drive the adoption of edge analytics. Edge analytics involves processing and analyzing data at the edge of the network, closer to the data source, rather than sending it to centralized systems. This approach reduces latency, enhances real-time decision-making, and minimizes bandwidth requirements. Edge analytics will find applications in areas like manufacturing, healthcare, logistics, and smart cities.

h. Data Governance and Quality Management: With the increasing reliance on data analytics, organizations will emphasize data governance and quality management. Effective data governance frameworks ensure data integrity, security, and compliance, while quality management processes focus on ensuring data accuracy, completeness, and reliability. Establishing robust data governance and quality management practices will be essential to derive meaningful insights and maintain trust in analytics outcomes.

i. Industry-Specific Analytics Solutions: Business analytics will become more tailored to specific industries and domains. Industry-specific analytics solutions will emerge, incorporating industry-specific data models, metrics, and algorithms. These solutions will address unique business challenges and provide specialized analytics capabilities for industries such as healthcare, finance, retail, manufacturing, and energy. These industry-specific solutions will enable businesses to gain deeper insights into their operations, identify industry-specific trends, and make more informed decisions.

j. Data Democratization: The trend of data democratization will continue to grow, aiming to make data and analytics accessible to a wider audience within organizations. Self-service analytics tools and platforms will empower business users across departments to access, analyze, and interpret data independently. This democratization of data will foster a data-driven culture, promote collaboration, and accelerate decision-making processes.

k. Quantum Computing: Although still in its early stages, quantum computing holds tremendous potential for advancing business analytics. Quantum computing's immense processing power and ability to handle complex algorithms can significantly enhance data analysis and optimization tasks. As quantum computing technology matures, businesses will explore its applications in areas like large-scale optimization problems, simulations, and cryptography.

l. Blockchain Analytics: With the growing adoption of blockchain technology, businesses will need specialized analytics tools to analyze and gain insights from blockchain data. Blockchain analytics can provide transparency, traceability, and auditing capabilities, helping businesses detect fraud, ensure compliance, and optimize supply chain processes. The ability to analyze blockchain data will become essential in industries like finance, logistics, and healthcare.

m. Social Media and Sentiment Analysis: Social media platforms generate vast amounts of user-generated content, presenting valuable opportunities for businesses to understand customer sentiment and trends. Sentiment analysis techniques will continue to evolve, enabling businesses to extract insights from social media data, online reviews, and customer feedback. Analyzing social media data will help businesses understand customer preferences, improve brand perception, and identify emerging market trends.

n. Cybersecurity Analytics: As cyber threats become more sophisticated, businesses will invest in cybersecurity analytics to detect and mitigate security breaches proactively. Cybersecurity analytics involves analyzing network traffic, user behavior, and system logs to identify anomalies, detect intrusions, and respond to cyber incidents effectively. By leveraging advanced analytics techniques and machine learning algorithms, businesses can strengthen their cybersecurity posture and protect sensitive data.

Overall, the future of business analytics will be shaped by advancements in artificial intelligence, machine learning, advanced data visualization, predictive and prescriptive analytics, real-time analytics, privacy and ethical considerations, natural language processing, augmented analytics, edge analytics, data governance and quality management, industry-specific solutions, data democratization, quantum computing, blockchain analytics, social media and sentiment analysis, and cybersecurity analytics. Embracing these trends and leveraging the power of analytics will enable businesses to gain valuable insights, make data-driven decisions, and stay competitive in an increasingly data-centric world.

www.ingramcontent.com/pod-product-compliance
Lightning Source LLC
Chambersburg PA
CBHW080547220526
45466CB00010B/3060